Dealing
with Doubt

Dealing with Doubt

When the Light Goes Out

Winkie Pratney

© 1989 by Winkie Pratney

Published by Fleming H. Revell
a division of Baker Book House Company
P.O. Box 6287, Grand Rapids, MI 49516-6287

Spire edition published 1998

Previously published under the title *The Thomas Factor* by Chosen Books

Printed in the United States of America

ISBN 0-8007-8650-5

For that solitary seeker
who braves the darkness
and dares believe.

In His favor is life . . .
"Weeping may endure for a night,
but joy comes in the morning."

                              Psalm 30:5

Contents

Introduction

"For You are my lamp, O Lord; The Lord shall enlighten my darkness."   2 Samuel 22:29

What in the World Is Going On?

We have been chosen by Jesus. We're walking with Him. Being His follower. Committed to doing what He says, being what He wants, going where He leads. But now, after all the years, we ask: Is it *real*?

"There has never been a time when it has been more difficult to be a Christian," says William Barclay, "and there has never been a time when it has been more necessary." At the edge of the new millennium, we now embark on what seems at once the most challenging, frightening, and exciting decade of contemporary history. Vast changes are taking place around the world. Russia. China. The Middle East. Entire political, economic, and military systems are shaking and altering before our very eyes. As we accelerate into the twenty-first century, we all face a time of major decisions. What is going to happen in our world? What is going to happen to us? If a caring, sovereign God is indeed in charge of the future, how can we best prepare to follow Him into it?

We are not the first to ask these questions. The early disciples also came to a time of great crisis and darkness. Jesus said He was going to die, that the Shepherd would be struck and all the sheep would be scattered. And then just when they most needed a sense of closeness, of common purpose and courage to face together what was coming, Jesus spoke to them about betrayal in their own ranks, about denial, about an immediate future they would all apparently have to face alone. And like us now on the edge of an incredible age, they were filled with questions.

"Thomas said to Him, 'Lord, we do not know where You are going, and how can we know the way?' "(John 14:5).

What did Jesus mean? Where was He going? What were they supposed to do now? They had general assurances from the Lord before, but this time was really serious; and the person who dared voice to Jesus his unspoken questions was not satisfied with a general promise.

We all know Thomas, don't we? The disciple who doubted. Thomas, the born skeptic with the heart of a scientist, the man who said even after the miracle: "Unless I can put my hand in the hole in His side I will not believe."

There has never been a time in contemporary Christianity when the temptation of Thomas was so prevalent and wide-spread at all levels of the Church. We, especially of the Western world, live in a period of deep uneasiness in the Christian Church. While some is obviously fallout from scandals, the failures of well-known people, ministries, and institutions, there is another factor at work deeper than this. Even our culture currently reflects a mood of pessimism, malaise, and disenchantment.

The Church is experiencing a time of great change; a "whole lot of shaking," forsaking, and breaking is going on. There is an inability in most people to get a handle on what is happening personally or globally. The questions of Thomas are ours as we face the immediate future: What is God up to? What is happening to me? What can I do in the midst of all this?

The River Is Rising—Toward 2001 A.D.

Our answer may be found in a vision given to the prophet Ezekiel. In the vision a man took him out into a river, farther and farther until he could no longer stand on his own.

In the twenty-fifth year of our captivity . . . [the Lord] took me into the land of Israel and set me on a very high mountain. . . . There was a man whose appearance was like the appearance of bronze . . . a measuring rod in his hand. . . . The man said to me, "Son of man, look with your eyes and hear with your ears, and fix your mind on everything I show you."   Ezekiel 40:1–4

There followed lengthy and specific instructions for the reconstruction of the Temple and the city of Jerusalem. Then this:

He brought me back to the door of the house; and behold, water was flowing from under the threshold of the house toward the east, for the house faced east. And the water was flowing down from under, from the right side of the house, from south of the altar.

And he brought me out by way of the north gate and led me around on the outside to the outer gate by way of the gate that faces east. And behold, water was trickling from the south side. When the man went out toward the east with a line in his hand, he measured a thousand cubits, and he led me through the water, *water reaching the ankles.*

Again he measured a thousand and led me through the water, *water reaching the knees.* Again he measured a thousand and led me through the water, *water reaching the loins.*

Again he measured a thousand; and *it was a river that I could not ford, for the water had risen,* enough water to swim in, a river that could not be forded. And he said to me, "Son of man, have you seen this?"   Ezekiel 47:1–6, NAS

This vision is not only a promise of God's inheritance for Israel; it is also a metaphor of increasing risk, of inevitable major changes in our Christian life, the "passages" of spiritual growth. The Church especially in the West is in what seems perhaps the most difficult and frightening level. We have learned to live in comparative security with water around both our ankles and our knees, but now things are getting serious. God is bringing us into life and healing, but first we have to get where we no longer move in the water but the water moves us. This is the task of the man with the measuring line; this is the intention of God for our time.

A Prelude

And he showed me a pure river of water of life, clear as crystal, proceeding from the throne of God and of the Lamb. In the middle of its street, and on either side of the river, was the tree of life, which bore twelve fruits, each tree yielding its fruit every month. And the leaves of the tree were for the healing of the nations.   Revelation 22:1–2

The Waters of Life

To understand the changes God is bringing to our lives—and to find answers to our doubts—we need first to see how much of life from creation to the present day has to do with water. Scripture speaks of water as a life-giving stream:

> These waters issue out toward the east country, and go down into the desert, and go into the sea: which being brought forth into the sea, the waters shall be healed. And it shall come to pass, that every thing that liveth, which moveth, whithersoever the rivers shall come, shall live: and there shall be a very great multitude of fish, because these waters shall come thither: for they shall be healed; and every thing shall live whither the river cometh. Ezekiel 47:8–9, KJV

It is significant that much of life in creation, in the Scriptures, and in our current physical existence has to do with water. Earth, of all the planets in our solar system, perhaps in all God's universe, is the dominantly water-rich world. Oceans cover two-thirds of our planet. Rain feeds the fertilization cycle and keeps the multiple billions of plants and trees alive. Snow caps our poles and puts some of our world to sleep in winter; rivers, lakes, and streams become a source of refreshment and joy in the heat of summer.

Water is in Scripture a symbol of both life and death. Take Christian baptism, for instance; the image of water signifies both burial and resurrection (new life). During my early years of ministry I had so many backsliders and dropouts as a result of my ineffective witnessing that I thought, *Well, perhaps I should baptize them. I'll hold them under twice and take them out once! I won't get to heaven, but they will.*

Water dominates our whole lives. We commence our physical birth when "the waters burst." A large percentage of the physical body is made up of water. Every major cell, tissue, and lean muscle mass is replete with water. We can go weeks without food but only a few days without water; dehydration invariably means death.

The birth and death of early earth is likewise filled with references to water; the Bible speaks of the waters "above" and "under" (Genesis 1:7) and of God's gathering the waters together (Genesis 1:9–10). God even speaks to the waters in the creation of life (Genesis 1:20–22).

Some creation scientists postulate that before the early earth was destroyed, it had both a water layer in its upper atmosphere and perhaps another modulating water layer around its core. This early earth may not have been struck by the directly unscreened rays of the sun. It may instead have been warmed from its core, an energy source something like a perfectly balanced breeder reactor, gently moderating its heat to the surface.

According to these creation scientists the destruction of the world took place like this: God spoke in judgment to the center of the earth and unbalanced that reactor. It overloaded; sections of earth cracked like a microwaved egg. That water-moderator shell shot up in places under tremendous, intense pressure. Huge, violent explosions of water cracked the floating granite substructure layer of our planet. Fountains of water as high as two or three miles devastated an upper firmament shell loaded with electromagnetic energy and it in turn discharged onto the surface of the doomed early world.

If this is the way it happened, can you imagine how utterly scary it was? In places like the Paluxy River you can still see authenticated dinosaur tracks and what appear to be apparently large human tracks trapped in the same disaster together. The prints are stretched out. There is a human handprint still left of a scrabbling, panicky attempt to get up after a fall. The tracks sometimes cross, but the lizards are apparently not after the people. Everybody's running . . . going in different directions. Everyone is running from something that is scaring the living daylights out of them.

Can you imagine what it would be like to see for the very first time the utter blackness of space and the discharge of lightning like at no other time in earth history? And then, for the first time in the record of mankind, rain. Rain that washed down out of the skies along with subterranean explosions of water that sent giant tidal waves sweeping over the shallow land masses in the awful judgment of the first world. Water: life and death. It was true in the days of Noah. That first flood that destroyed the wicked ancient world also preserved eight people, carried by the waves in the shelter of God.

And so it goes throughout Scripture. There is Moses, the greatest of the Old Testament Law-giving figures. His life is marked, both life and death, by water. Pharaoh commands all Hebrew parents: "Throw your male babies into the water" (Exodus 1:22). Moses has parents who, besides being law-abiding Hebrews, are somewhat imaginative. Fearing God, they look for a creative alternative way to carry out the king's command, and come up with a literal interpretation of the law that certainly meets with God's approval. After all, Pharaoh didn't say *how* to throw the baby into the water . . . so they put him into a little boat (Exodus 2:3) and you know the rest of the story.

The life of Moses is spared by the same water that means

death to so many other babies. Later, he meets his wife through water (Exodus 2:16–21). The spared child becomes a wanted, hunted man; and that man is at last called by God to lead the children of Israel through the waters of the Red Sea, which close down on pursuing Egypt and drown Pharaoh and his hosts (Exodus 14:21–31).

Water: life to Israel, death to Pharaoh. Water also marks the end of Moses' earthly ministry. On the edge of the promise, he strikes the rock of symbol in anger instead of speaking to it. Unable to enter the Promised Land during his lifetime, Moses is buried by God in the desert to await the fulfillment of His original promise. Moses has to wait to enter the Promised Land thousands of years later, when in his resurrection he joins Jesus on the Mount of Transfiguration (Matthew 17:1–5). Life and death by water.

In Ezekiel's vision, we see a rising river of water. He is taken out farther and farther; and level by level the water encompasses him. Four areas this water touches: the ankles, the knees, the loins, and, finally, everything.

There is the man with the measuring line. Did you ever notice in some sections of the Bible how much space is given to apparently useless and boring measurements? Chapters of it! When I first began to study it, I couldn't see the sense of it. I thought, *What a waste! Why didn't God put in more verses like Psalm 23 and John 3:16 instead of all this cubits stuff?* But then I never did like measurements much.

Yet it is obvious that God is a Counter, a Measurer. He not only measures things like this river, the Tabernacle, and the great City to come; He counts the days, the people, the tears, the sins of the world. In Psalm 147:4 we read that God numbers the stars. He even names them all. In Matthew 10:30 we read that even the hairs on your head are numbered! God seems to be into numbers.

Now there are some missionary people who are not only good at speaking or singing or writing; they are also good at engineering and carpentry and building. They can build both a church and a place to put the church. I find such people embarrassing. I can't even put a shelf up straight on the wall!

In my more rational moments between smashed thumbs and wasted materials I think about the factors that make people good builders. I know at least one thing they have that I don't. They habitually think of precise measurement; the first thing they pull out is a tape measure, while the first thing I reach for is a saw. They measure six times and cut once; I measure no times at all and have to cut 150 times! The difference between me and my kinds of attempts and a real carpenter, builder, or craftsman is called measurement and attention to detail.

We have a God who counts stars and comes to the funeral of every sparrow and this God is *infinitely detailed.* We tend to think of the general greatness, immensity, and compassing power of God, but He is also precise. The same God who has upheld the galaxies effortlessly for light-years both knows and cares how many hairs you lost this morning.

So that man walks in the vision and measures. See how slowly the water rises. Only to the ankles after a thousand measures! Nothing very fast. Some things change very slowly. And in this vision, the man walks out a thousand cubits before the river rises to his ankles. A thousand cubits. If we consider a cubit eight inches long, we're talking about 15,000 feet! That's a long way to walk to have water just reach the ankles.

We are perhaps unaccustomed to this kind of slowness. Most of us grew up to like, to prefer instant things. We belong to a generation used to watching T.V. programs with anything slow and boring edited out. We like things to happen fast. We eat fast, drive fast, live life in the fast lane. We want our miracles of provision, healing, or restoration to happen instantly.

Thus, we are not so sure of supernatural things that happen very gradually. How can we see them unless they move quickly?

We may be in a terrible situation and want things changed

immediately. Of course, the same God who turned water into wine instantly can do it again, but a lot of times He moves much more slowly. After all, He turns water into wine all the time. He does this millions of times all over the world every year through His creation, grapes, but we often fail to appreciate that this, too, is a work of God. It is only when He accelerates time and shrinks His power to our level of perception that we are compelled to notice His help and intervention. George MacDonald said, "The miracles of Jesus were His Father's normal works, wrought small and swift that we might see them."

The slow change can be a miracle, too. Someone can look back and say, "That was a mess a year ago. Back then I had no idea how it could ever be any different." But little by little, things changed. It *is* better now than it was before. He has been at work even when we have not been looking. Fractionally the tide has risen, and now there is water where once there was only mud and sand. God has made all these changes in us and we have cause to be thankful for the slow miracle as well as the fast. As the old lady said, "Well, I ain't now what I *should* be, and I ain't yet what I'm *gonna* be, but praise God, I at least ain't *what I was!*"

And you, too, need never be the same. It is time to begin the scary, costly change. Come with me now. We are going to a place of both life and death. We are going down to the river.

Dealing
with Doubt

Level One

Water to the Ankles

"Lord, we do not know where You are going; how do we know the way?"
—Thomas questions Jesus

When the man went out toward the east with a line in his hand, he measured a thousand cubits, and he led me through the water, water reaching the ankles.   Ezekiel 47:3, NAS

1

Healing from Chaos

The first miracle of the early Church after Pentecost had to deal with the healing of someone's ankles. It centered around a man who had been *born* lame; he had never walked in his life (Acts 3:1–16). When the disciples met him, he was at the Beautiful Gate begging for alms. He looked at Peter and John, expecting something from them. "I do not possess silver and gold," said Peter, "but what I do have I give to you." And the power of the Resurrected Christ touched the lame man in the ankles; God healed him instantly. He called out for "alms" but in the name of Jesus, Peter and John gave him "legs" instead!

In our spiritual journeys, all of us begin at the bottom. There really has been a "fall," not only in our world but in us, too. We both bear the consequences and reinforce the choices of our first sinning parents, and the devastating harvest that has resulted over the centuries is now the current tragedy of our world. No one who knows the meaning of the Bible word *lost* needs any illustration of this primary truth; our first and greatest need is to be *found*, at the deepest and most basic levels of our being.

In M. Scott Peck's probing book on community and peace-making, *A Different Drum*, he refers to an excellent recent university study on six stages of spiritual experience. These stages are not only apparently universal; they seem also to me to have peculiar relevance at this time to the Church in the Western world. Peck reduces these various stages to four ascending levels of experience: what he calls *chaos*, *tradition*, *doubt*, and *mystery*.

The four basic transitional stages or passages of spiritual experience bear a natural correspondence to the four rising levels of Ezekiel's vision of the river: waters first to the ankles (chaos), then to the knees (tradition), to the loins (doubt), and to swim in (mystery).

Let us examine each stage of our spiritual growth as a parallel to the vision of the river. In our lives, too, there will be a river of God from the Temple; at each measure we will come to see and touch a whole new level of spiritual experience. You can think of these if you like as passages of the spirit, necessary levels through which we all must pass in our adventure with God.

Peck calls the first stage of our lives before conversion *chaos*. It's a pretty good description, if we take it in its common meaning and not confuse it with "randomness." Within the last few decades the word *chaos* has become the term for a whole new science, a term to describe patterns discovered in the underlying complex simplicity of nature. The science of chaos has become a way of seeing structure in the apparent disorder of different things like clouds and coastlines, waves and leaves, a dripping tap in your bathroom or a swirling storm on a planet like Jupiter millions of miles away. Chaos in nature is now a study of unity in diversity and order in disorder, replete with odd names like *Koch Curves*, *Lorentz Attractors*, and *Mandelbrot Sets*.

Put simply, this recent discipline says that nothing in life is as simple as it seems. The complex diversity of things is often at heart the result of tiny changes in initial conditions on which the result is sensitively dependent. The new science of chaos has shown that in life, randomness is death; that small things can make a big difference later; and that a complex system can be turbulent and coherent at the same time.

Coherent, yet turbulent. Like you, like me. *Chaos.* All of us know what it is like to live a life that, for all its apparent order, is nevertheless antisocial, adult autistic, and devotedly self-centered—another word for what Barry McGuire called his early life without Christ: "Insanity."

Chaos is a good description for a life in which we have become dangerously irresponsible, so captive to sin and self-deception that we become pawns of our own choices, circumstances, or conditions. In a life of willful rebellion against God, we like to think of ourselves as free. But look closely and you see we are locked into repeating patterns, not truly random, but endlessly repeating. Like the man at the gate of the Temple, we see no real way out of our situation. Maybe we are frustrated, immobilized, helplessly locked down into our own intensifying, recurring patterns of guilt, blame, and self-pity, really wanting something better but wholly unable to get up by our own strength. Crippled, unclean, demeaned, and demoralized, we fight having to admit the final truth: We can do nothing at last but perhaps humble ourselves enough to beg for help and mercy.

This is the place of need for the first stage of spiritual growth. It involves the "waters to the ankles." What is the significance of water that begins at the feet? It means that God will come first to restore in our lives the following things:

(1) *Purity:* He makes us clean.

(2) *Dignity:* He gives us a real self-worth.

(3) *Responsibility:* He restores to us a sense of commitment and care.

(4) *Mobility:* He empowers us to reach out to help others.

Purity

The river of God washes first at our ankles. There is a key significance of that first water contact with the feet in Scripture, one we tend to forget in the world of paved roads, carpets, and socks and shoes. Our feet are the parts of us that are most in touch with the earth. We take off our shoes when we draw near the bush that burns with fire, because we are on holy ground. That's why the footwashing ceremony of Bible times was such an important part of honoring a guest at your home; it was a provision for cleansing.

And there is first a cleansing for our sin in the river. In his eventual obedience to God, Naaman, the proud Syrian general, was freed in the river from leprosy, the AIDS of his time. "Wash me thoroughly from my iniquity, and cleanse me from my sin," prayed a repentant David. "Wash me, and I shall be whiter than snow" (Psalm 51:2, 7). Into our guilty, chaotic, and defiled lives comes the river of God, cleansing and purifying. Our first contact with the river comes with the conviction that we cannot cleanse ourselves, and that we must be touched by His mercy: "Not by works of righteousness which we have done, but according to His mercy He saved us, through the washing of regeneration and renewing of the Holy Spirit" (Titus 3:5). The Bible also speaks of the Church being purified "with the washing of water by the word" (Ephesians 5:26). We walk through the world and we get our feet dirty. And in our day, the spiritual reality is the same. For our daily contact with a fallen world we need daily cleansing from the waterbowl of Christ.

Dignity

The second great accomplishment of salvation is the sense of value and specialness it restores to men and women. "You are a chosen generation," says 1 Peter 2:9, "a royal priesthood, a holy nation, His own special people, that you may proclaim the praises of Him who called you out of darkness into His marvelous light." A lame man has lost more than his legs; the loss of his mobility is also an assault on his dignity.

There is something about an external handicap that gets inside you; when you can no longer use your own limbs you tend also to lose your desire to do anything else.

John's Gospel records the account of healing of another crippled man (John 5:1–15). Jesus meets a man utterly powerless to move, someone unable to walk for 38 years. Day after day he has been carried there by others, perhaps even drags himself there to the sheep market pool, one small, lame part of the great crowd that hangs around Bethesda hoping for a miracle. I have friends who like this man have lost their ability to walk; I can know only something of the daily battle they wage with frustration and anger, the sense of uselessness, impotence, and helpless dependence such a crippling brings to the spirit. Thirty-eight years. "What more can we say about him," said Luigi Santucci, "once we know this about him? What is there to say about such a man apart from the number of years?"

And Jesus asks what must have sounded like a silly sort of question: "Do you want to be cured?" Cured? After being dragged here year after eternal year, always watching for the moving of the waters, scrabbling toward the rim of the pool at the troubling touch of the angel, but always being beaten to the edge by the man with the crippled hand but the healthy big elbows, the blind man with 20/20 hearing of water motion, or the deaf Olympic pole-vaulter?

Yet here is a Man with a question to ask that is not at all silly when you have been sick so long. "Do you want to be well?"

Sometimes you lose hope. One by one, your friends have gotten tired of carrying you around. They don't call anymore and you can't blame them. Nobody wants to look at you; they are afraid you will capture them with your naked stare of need. "I have no man" is your life summary now; you are all you've got but even you can't stand to live with yourself. And as for the angel who sometimes stirs these waters, how come he never notices you? You've been coming now year after year and here you are, still crippled while others have walked away free. Some healing angel! The angel must be blind.

But now suddenly a Face that does not look away; a gaze of utter and total attention; a look that will not let you go. Jesus is looking at you with those eyes that have eternity in them. And He is speaking, not to the crowd but to you. *"Do you want to be well?"*

Sometimes you forget what it ever felt like to feel good. You no longer remember what it is to be ordinary. You do not pray in faith because you have no remaining vision of what normal is. Your problem so fills the horizon of your daily life you have no room anymore for a surprise sunrise. Maybe you have been sick so long that now in your heart of hearts you actually find it preferable just to stay that way. You tried before; it never happened. It happened to others; it never happened to you. *"Do you want to be well?"* asks Jesus. *"Do you?"*

Responsibility

It is a frightening thing to be well. Ask the man in the asylum about it. Ask the habitual offender who is checked once again into his prison home how he handled the latest venture outside. It is sometimes easier to be sick. When you are well, people expect things from you. They expect you to help others. They expect you to carry your share of the burden, to be part of the solution and not the problem, to have something you can give for a change. When you are well, you are to be a healing force yourself in society; you are someone whom others may want to come to and draw from. It is a very serious question, this one Jesus asks by the edge of the water, as it reaches for our crippled ankles: "Do you *really* want to be well?" "It's not my fault," says the cripple at the edge of the pool. "I have no man." *"I am a Man,"* says the presence of Jesus. *"Rise, take up your bed and walk."*

Mobility

Purity, dignity, responsibility. And when the healing river of God touches the lame man at the Gate Beautiful it gives him the one thing every person needs who cannot move: mobility. The man at the gate has much more than a divine healing; he also experiences a miracle. It is indeed a "notable" miracle because Scripture makes it clear that he has *never* walked. A man, around forty years old, instantly learning to walk? No tripping around, no crawling, no stumbling as a baby does? Just like that? A miracle indeed.

So comes the river of God to us in our powerlessness, in our weakness, in our helplessness, in our irresponsibility, having always to be carried by other people. The river touches us. It sets us on our feet. It sends us out with a message for a crippled world. It makes every Christian a missionary and everyone else a mission field.

When the priests bearing the Ark of God came to cross the Jordan into the Promised Land, the waters marking the beginning of their mission did not part until their feet touched the river (Joshua 3:7–17). And they stood on their feet in the middle of that riverbed with the waters rising "in a heap" in a faraway city until the whole nation had passed over to the other side. When the priests' feet then touched dry ground, the waters refilled the riverbed to overflowing.

This divine commission to move out may take us to some scary places. The water now washing our ankles will rise much more, and if we go where it is headed we will travel with it to a parched and dying world.

There is a mighty *GO* in the word *Gospel*. What cleansed, restored, and made you caring now needs to be taken to the rest of the world; the river brings healing and life wherever it flows, and a great draught of fish. Mobility. The Great Commission in our generation is a realizable goal. We know what it will take. We know what needs to be done. It can happen. We have begun to focus on the untouched places that are the last great frontiers of missions; God is looking for those who will go.

Maybe you never understood just what it meant to get involved with Jesus Christ when you first said you would follow. But He is out first of all to make you clean, to give you beauty for ashes, real love for others, and a global task to do that will not be over until you stand face-to-face before His throne.

What about the countries that are closed to the Gospel? "What about them?" says Brother Andrew. "There are no closed doors. Show me a country closed to the Gospel and I will show you a way to get in. I may not be able to tell you how to get back. But after all, Jesus just said, 'Go.' He didn't say, 'Come back.'"

All this and more is involved when the first innocent wave curls at your ankles. Are you ready for the rest of the river?

Prayer

Lord, we thank You for the bittersweet memories of things once deeply loved and shared that have now passed into history and the record of our walk with You. We thank You for each one of them—the places, the people, the circumstances and situations that became for a small, sweet time the reflection of Your great grace and provision for us.

We appreciate in each of them Your care; we acknowledge in all of them Your dear hand; we rejoice in what each taught us of Your beauty and Your bounty. And now that they are gone, moved with some sadness into the journal of what is now forever past, we ask for the grace to lift our hearts and our hands from what may never be again to what is yet to come. Our brook has dried up; the birds You sent are now gone, but we are not forsaken or forgotten. We hear again that still, small voice that calls on us once more to touch and taste and see anew the adventure that comes with Your friendship, our living and Creator God.

Thank You, then, Lord, for what is now past; we look to You in faith for the needs of the present hour in newness of expectation; and we say "Welcome" to the future as something under Your care, as that which has been filtered through the righteousness, care, and faithfulness of a God who cannot lie, who shall not fail, and who has promised never to leave or forsake us. We affirm again that nothing You give us can or must ever take Your own lovely place. You are our Father, and we are glad.

Level Two

Water to the Knees

"My Lord and my God."   —Thomas surrenders to Jesus

Again he measured a thousand and led me through the water, water reaching the knees.   Ezekiel 47:4, NAS

2

The Discipline of Limits

The river comes, secondly, to the knees. At this second level I can't help but think of an image from the wholly irreverent movie *Monty Python and the Holy Grail*. One unforgettable image from this weird flick is of the Black Knight protecting the bridge. He challenges King Arthur, who after a short scuffle promptly hacks off one of the Black Knight's arms. "Just a flesh wound," the Knight mutters and undaunted resumes the battle. Arthur then proceeds to systematically cut off his other arm and both his legs. Finally, there is left this man hopping precariously on his knees yelling: "*All right. Let's call it a draw.*"

It ought to be obvious. You can't fight when you are reduced to your knees. Resistance on this level is futile. The whole heart of the bowed knee in Scripture has to do with the idea of submission.

In the first stage of a standard spiritual conversion, a person goes from what Peck calls "chaos" to some form of "tradition," some structure, some limits. For example, you've been "doing your own thing" in some sophisticated or unsophisticated way. Then the river comes; it touches your ankles, it cleanses you and gives you strength. It puts you back on your feet. It makes you strong. Now you have some dignity; now you have some mobility. And with that dignity and mobility comes a danger. The danger is that now you've become a motivated person, you can easily become *self*-motivated. Now that you can move on your own, you may do just that outside of God.

The danger then of God's making us significant and responsible is that we now are tempted to do as we please. We can call it "the Protestant heresy" because it comes only to people who are free. We can be *too* free. Our liberty can degenerate into license.

That's why law is important and why tradition is important. That's why at weddings a bride doesn't usually come down in a purple dress with green spots, exchange chickens with the groom, and have a local dogcatcher conduct the ceremony. There is ancient wisdom, significant heritage embodied even in many of our traditional customs and rituals and ceremonies. There are principles. We need rules and limits and boundaries.

So the next thing is for the river to touch our knees. We now have to learn to do things simply because we're told, not because we personally agree, understand, or think that it's a good idea. We have to learn to obey even when the call comes against our own best intentions and our own good ideas.

Most conversions take place in this transition from chaos to tradition, nothingness to order. Even in the religious world that is not Christian, this is an observable stage of change: from dissipation to discipline; from doing our own thing to doing what we are told. The guy who's a drug addict takes up Zen Buddhism (with or without "motorcycle maintenance"). Before perhaps he was a vomiting, addicted transsexual; now he chants koans while people slap him on the back with wooden boards if he moves. The dissolute, indolent playboy who wouldn't give you the time of day before 11:45 A.M. now chants a mantra faithfully at his 4:00 A.M. devotions. Then after his sparse vegetarian breakfast he is off to sell magazines or flowers in airports.

This change is especially true in *real* conversion. What we get at this level are some limits and some guidelines. We all need rules. If we find the right ones (from God's Book and in God's world) and work with them, we are working with life as God designed it. And most times we're comfortable in this. The point to notice as the water laps around our knees is that now we do what we are told, rather than following our usual inclination to do what we think or feel. Previously, if people didn't like the way we were, then tough; we weren't in this world to measure up to their expectations and they weren't in this world to measure up to ours, and if by chance we met, it was beautiful. Now it's all changed. We are given rules, the limits, the way it's done; and we learn to bow the knee.

This surrender is, as we will find, a place of real security. We are told what to do by a trusted authority. We learn principles. We learn there are reasons behind the rules, and we learn the rules themselves and commit ourselves to God in them. We learn God's laws, His structures that govern relationships in the home and family and marriage, in business and government. We delight as a culture in seeing how God put things together and discussing why we think He did. Seminars that propose to show us these rules and relationships are a key part of our information-centered Western world.

But God likes people who do things because He told them to, not because they always understand why. Brother Andrew said he noticed one key difference between people who served God in the Bible and people who claim to serve God today. The people in the Bible disagreed with God quite vocally but still did what He said. Today we agree wholeheartedly with God, but *don't* do what He says.

The Bible God is the Ruler of the universe. All our lives are dependent on His care and guidance. He is under no obligation, save His love, to speak or reveal Himself to anyone. We, however, are dependent on revelation, and revelation is given only in trust. George Washington Carver, the man who found God's hidden treasures in the lowly peanut plant, said, "When you love someone or something long enough, it will reveal its secrets to you."

There is a divine order even to the *way* we receive truth from God. It goes something like this:

Revelation	— God speaks
Practical Service	— We do it
Illumination	— He explains it (maybe!)

This communication order is inherent in all of God's dealings with mankind; it is illustrated even in the order of the languages of Scripture. Hebrew, the language of the Old Testament, is a revelation/action language. Greek, the primary language of the New Testament, is one better suited to description and explanation. This is an order that promotes faith and develops trust with an ever-growing wonder.

The *maybe* in the above diagram is important. Explanation is not our own option. God never *has* to explain it. Obedience always precedes illumination. A. W. Tozer put it like this: "Obedience is the opener of the eyes."

It is true that we have to be sure it really *is* God speaking. It is biblically true that we are to "test all things" (1 Thessalonians 5:21), and to "test the spirits" (1 John 4:1). It is also true that the Christian life is supposed to be the wisest way, one that demands the commitment not only of the whole heart but also of the mind. God has not called us to some careless leap in the dark. God never said, "Be ye transformed by the removal of your minds."

But it is not true that God has to explain things to us before we can obey Him. It is not true that we have to know why before we must do it. God has an order in the way He communicates with us, and that order is always this: He speaks; we do it; He explains it—*maybe*. If we attempt to reverse this divine order we get into serious trouble.

Yet reverse it we do. We do it all the time. We do it especially in the Western world, with our rich heritage of thought from civilizations like those of Greece and India and millennia of philosophy, education, and science. It is the characteristic idolatry of our communication/information culture that our lust to understand has time and time again stood in the way of the clear Word of God. Our educational system, even in the majority of our best Bible colleges, fits this inversion. *FIRST we explain. Then we're encouraged to do. Later we are expected to become godly.* Yet somehow this "spiritual" goal keeps receding for many. They can't understand why the more they seem to learn, the less they seem to grow. In the desire to understand, we have become the victims of our own strength.

It is not the facts or the learning that is the problem. If the more we learn the less we grow in trust, then ignorance is indeed bliss. The less we know the happier we will be, and heaven is a final haven for all true idiots. If it is true that the more we know the less thrilled we are, then God Himself (with infinite wisdom) should rightfully be infinitely bored. If learning is an impediment to spiritual growth and excitement, then the Lord Jesus Himself who "increased in wisdom and stature" (Luke 2:52) as time went on should have become less and less committed to His task. Yet He was a man who lived by the hour, whose whole life was a testament of dangerous and infectious joy and of whom it was said near the end of His mission, "The zeal for Your house has eaten me up."

No, knowledge is not the problem; what we have is a *wrong priority.* Something good and right has been put in the wrong place and given false authority—a nice, approved, and eminently respectable idol, but an idol nevertheless.

What actually happens when we reverse the divine order is an eventual erosion of faith, a "rust" in our trust! The result of this inverted approach in our spiritual lives is that we become more cynical and rationalistic and fault-finding.

More than a hundred years ago, one of the great revivalists of history, Charles Finney, noticed the danger of a minister's explaining too much before calling people to obedience to

God. He said that this tendency would eventually result in a generation with a critical, proud, and rationalistic mindset that "either has no real faith or holds most loosely to Divine things that do not admit of a clear explanation" (*Reflections on Revival*). If God is not going to explain to our single brain cells why He made the universe, well, then, we're not going to do what He says.

The Western world (which leads in information and communication technology) has done precisely this. Part of God's work in our time is to restore divine order to our lives, to learn again how to follow when we cannot see.

This is exactly why God taught the leaders of His people in Bible days the central thought of *covenant*: that God and man may enter into a mutual pledge of faithfulness and commitment. In Genesis 15:18 and 17:4 the Lord covenants with Abram, promising his children not only the land from the rivers of Egypt to the Euphrates, but to make him "a father of many nations." To Noah and his family on the edge of the world's greatest disaster, God's covenants are the safety of the ark and His promise never again to destroy all life on earth by flood (Genesis 8:21; 9:11). His token of this was a rainbow (Genesis 9:13).

To "cut a covenant" in those ancient days in the cultures from which Israel came meant the forging of a mutual pact or oath made deeply serious by the slaying and sacrifice of an animal. This idea was inherent: "May my blood be spilled like this and my body cut apart if I ever break this promise to you." It also sometimes involved the sharing of a meal with someone; you would never harm even your worst enemy who shared your table.

What did covenant with God mean to Israel in Moses' day? It involved *blood* (Exodus 24:8), a *book* (Exodus 24:7), and a serious *bond* that was never to be broken. He told them, "If you will indeed obey My voice and keep My covenant, then you shall be a special treasure to Me above all people; for all the earth is Mine" (Exodus 19:5). They were warned not to covenant with the cultures around them, nor with their gods (Exodus 23:32). And for His part God promised that "before all your people I will do marvels such as have not been done in all the earth, nor in any nation; and all the people among whom you are shall see the work of the Lord. For it is an awesome thing that I will do with you" (Exodus 34:10). To this day Israel celebrates its Sabbath in honor of that covenant made so long ago (Exodus 31:16).

We have today in Christ by the "blood of the everlasting covenant" the promised help of the full energy of the God-head for those who trust Him. This is the significance of the Lord's Supper when He took bread, broke it, and said, "This is My body which was broken for you," and poured out the wine with the words, "This is the blood of the New Covenant in My name." Jesus is committed to me by His blood, by His Book, and by an utterly serious mutual bond: God Himself has bound Himself to my happiness as I have bound myself to His.

Covenant also means this: It may be no great thing for me to give my trust and promises to God, but it is wondrous indeed that God would entrust His promises to me. My faithfulness to God will always be limited by my finiteness and humanity, but His faithfulness to me is without limit and without measure.

A classic example of faithfulness to God while enduring the discipline of limits is Joseph. If ever someone held onto a dream that seemed doomed from the start it was he. From his story, which we will explore in the next chapter, we will see that God is faithful beyond our understanding, that even when our dreams seem to self-destruct, God keeps His Word.

3

Joseph in Egypt: When Your Dreams Self-Destruct

There is a certain hard reality about getting your feet wet. Water can chill. And what happens to a high and lofty dream when it is hit by the cold water of reality? Those cold waves life's river throws at you can be devastating. How do the promises of God square with the failure of someone close to you whom you trusted, the pressures of seduction, temptation, and compromise, or, perhaps the hardest of all, to be apparently completely forgotten? What do you do with a wave that seems to leave you threatened in all the places you have just seen made strong—your dignity, your freedom, your purity, and your calling in God?

Years ago people used to sing a lot about dreams. In New Zealand we had a great deal of music from Europe and the United States. There were songs like Cliff Richards' "Theme for a Dream," the Everly Brothers' "Dream," and Johnny Burnette's "Dreamin'."

The last few years, things have changed and we don't hear so much singing about dreams anymore. Can it be that the world has lost its dreams? Many think the American dream has turned into the American nightmare. People used to write about utopias; they believed they would build a new world, a wonderful world where everything would be rosy. That's been ruined in the last few years. Wars ruined it. The Bomb ruined it. Ongoing sin ruined it. The Brave New World is still afraid and still the same.

Humanists used to go out with stars in their eyes and say, "Man will build a new world." Malcolm Muggeridge was such a person. He believed that given the right technology, the right education, people would be beautiful. He became bitterly disillusioned with his humanism and became a Christian. The world today is being broken and smashed in its dreams. The Optimistic Eighties have become the Nervous Nineties.

I once disliked witnessing to artists about Christ. I could speak to scientists because my background is organic research chemistry. I could share with musicians because I had a rock band for three and a half years. But I could not witness to artists. I thought artists were weird. I couldn't understand what they were trying to say.

One day the Lord spoke to my heart. He said, *Son, do you love artists?* I said, "Well, yes, of course I love artists. Thou knowest I lovest all men." So He asked again: *Do you love artists?* "No," I said. "Actually, I don't. I think they are all weird."

The Lord said, *I am an artist.*

"Well, all artists are weird—except You, Lord."

I began to realize there was an entire culture of people that I'd shut out because I didn't believe they could really be affected by the power of God like the other people I had seen. God convicted me of lack of love and concern for them. It's very easy to shut out an entire culture. Somebody's hair is longer or shorter than yours, or he has a safety pin through his cheek, and you say, "I don't know if God can save him."

So I began to pray. I took up photography—that's a science of optics and chemistry and yet an art, too. It helped link the world I knew with another world I didn't and bridged the gap. In a few months God began to open my eyes by visualizing through a camera lens some of the world of beauty He had made.

About a year later, I was sitting in San Francisco in a cafe. I looked on the wall and saw a painting. For the very first time in my life, I understood an artist. The artist had drawn a dry, barren world, with long grass that looked quite lifeless. Amidst that dead grass were two children; the grass around them was all short and stubbly. There was not a hint of green in the entire picture. The sky was dull and overcast, a brown, polluted yellow. The sun was only a big flat white penny spent in the sky; it didn't even shine, it was just there. There was a little girl standing in the grass and further back a little boy, almost lost in the grass. They both had these big eyes. The whole picture was brown—except for the blue in the kids' wide-open eyes. But instead of being a soft blue, the artist had chosen a hard, brilliant blue, like sapphire chips of glass.

Suddenly I understood what the artist was trying to say. "Here are two little ones; their eyes are wide open and they're seeing the whole world and it's dead. But you can see inside of them and they're dead, too. Just two little dead dolls stuck in a dead world."

And God spoke to me from that painting. He said, *When the dreams of children die, it's the end of the world.* When kids no longer have anything to believe in, they can't hope anymore. It's the end of the world.

In many people's lives, especially those who call themselves by the name of Jesus, there comes a time when dreams seem to die on you. People and circumstances and pressures conspire against what you are sure is God's calling. How can you handle the sins of others that affect your dreams? Take the story of Joseph.

Now Jacob dwelt in the land where his father was a stranger, in the land of Canaan. This is the genealogy of Jacob. Joseph, being seventeen years old, was feeding the flock with his brothers. And the lad was with the sons of Bilhah and the sons

of Zilpah, his father's wives; and Joseph brought a bad report
of them to his father.   Genesis 37:1–2

Joseph is a simple guy, childlike, imaginative, uncomplicated. He is ingenuous. Do you know anyone like Joseph?
Such people are becoming rare in our cynical, sophisticated,
media-weary world. They are so naïve and straightforward
that they can be embarrassing sometimes. They are the opposite of "cool," which is often a synonym for cynical, sophisticated, and cruel.

But Joseph watches his brothers blowing it and says, "Hey,
you guys! That's wrong! Hey, Dad, they're doing some wrong
things."

You can guess what his brothers think. They are disgusted
with him. Everybody knows it isn't cool to rat on people in
your family, even if they are doing wrong.

Some people say things and you have to ask, "Is that what
he meant or did he *actually* mean this? Does he say that
because he wants me to think that, but he really means the
opposite? Or does he say that because he *really* means that
and he means me to know that he means that?" We need to
study body language manuals and take police interrogation
courses to find out if people really mean what they say.

When you meet an ingenuous person, it's never like that.
Such encounters can be embarrassing! Arthur Katz, who has
a very regal bearing, visited our office and talked with my
secretary.

She said, "You're Art Katz."

"Yes."

"I thought you'd be different."

"Really?"

She said: "I thought you'd be taller."

He laughed. She blushed. Ingenuous. It's wonderful to
have a secretary like that around. Uncomplicated. Straightforward.

Joseph is like this. A person of integrity. Consistent. He

loves his father and his father loves him. This relationship is rare in the modern family.

One night God gives Joseph a dream. The next morning, having breakfast with his brothers, Joseph, in his simple but frank way, says, "Boy, did I ever have a neat dream last night. I can hardly believe it. Want to hear what it was about? We were all tying sheaves in the field and my sheaf stood up and all the other sheaves bowed before my sheaf." His brothers were not amused. "They hated him even more for his dreams and for his words" (Genesis 37:8).

It gets worse. He has another dream, and again uncool, ingenuous Joseph decides to share it with the whole family. "Hey!" says Joseph. "Remember that great dream God gave me? Well, you'll never believe it. Last night He gave me another one! Listen to this. You'll love it." And oblivious to the dark looks of his brothers he rattles on excitedly: "In this dream the sun and the moon and eleven stars bowed down to me. And, oh, Dad, the sun is you, the moon is you, Mom, and you guys are the eleven stars. Great, huh?"

Jacob, his dad, may not have been too swift, but he wasn't completely blind. Noticing the daggers in his sons' eyes, the father rebukes Joseph, saying, "What is this dream that you have dreamed? Shall your mother and I and your brothers indeed come to bow down to the earth before you?"

Who gives Joseph these dreams? *God* does. He shows him the same vision of his future in two different ways. There has never been a generation in history so visually sophisticated as this one. It is to this generation that the promise of God comes: "And it shall come to pass afterward that I will pour out My Spirit on all flesh; . . . *your old men shall dream dreams, your young men shall see visions*" (Joel 2:28, emphasis added).

A lot of people today are unable to distinguish between a call of God and religious fantasy. God speaks to the child heart, to the pure heart, to the heart set on seeking Him and loving Him. And if God gives you a dream, He will fulfill it.

I believe there are people to whom God has given dreams who today are wondering what in the world happened to them. God said to those people, "I have something for you that I am showing you," but then something seemed to go wrong and it's not clear exactly what. Look at Joseph.

His Brothers Betray Him

His father says, "Go take these peanut butter and jelly sandwiches down to your brothers." So along comes ingenuous Joseph with his sandwiches.

> When they saw him afar off, even before he came near them, they conspired against him to kill him. Then they said to one another, "Look, this dreamer is coming! Come therefore, let us now kill him and cast him into some pit; and we shall say, 'Some wild beast has devoured him.' We shall see what will become of his dreams!"
> Genesis 37:18–20

The oldest of the brothers, Reuben, hears these words and says, "Don't shed his blood, but cast him into the pit that is in the wilderness." Reuben thinks he might get him out later despite the murderous intentions of his brothers.

Did God really give Joseph a dream about everyone bowing down to him? If so, how come he's in a pit? How do you "bow down" to someone in a pit? What do you think Joseph thought?

Here is the first test of a dream: Can you handle it when even your own brothers (out of jealousy, envy, or just plain ignorance) oppose you and let you down?

An Ishmaelite trading party is going through on the way to Egypt. Joseph's brothers say to these Midianites: "Here's a good slave for you—strong and healthy. Make us an offer we can't refuse." They do. Reuben is away during that transaction but, perhaps out of fear, does not protest as the brothers kill an animal, dip Joseph's coat into the animal's blood, and take it back to their father who dearly loves his youngest son.

"This evil beast came and ate him up," they tell him. Jacob cries for a long time.

The most important thing to learn about a gift or calling of God is this: With great power always comes great responsibility. We all would like a dream from God, but are we prepared to handle the awesome responsibility that comes with it? We all would like the honor of representing Him, but are we prepared to be trained to think and act like Him? We talk about trusting God; can He trust us?

Only a godly character can survive the immense pressures a great dream brings with its promises. God is more concerned with how we handle pressure than with delivering us from pressure. Here are four false ways people respond when their dreams begin to evaporate:

1. Wildness (Intemperance). One of the most popular ways of dealing with the loss of a dream in the Western world is this: Go party it up and forget your sorrows. Joseph could have said to the Egyptians, "Give me a bottle of Nile Comfort. I never drank before, but since my world fell apart I may as well start now."

How do some people react to the apparent destruction of their dreams? They bury their pain in drugs. Grab themselves cans and bottles and get smashed out of their heads. Or shoot up. There are those pills that help them forget all ills. If they're short on cash, there's always a bag and glue.

The reaction of wildness is reaching new depths in our day, as so many young people are stripped not only of any sense of value or worth, but of hope. For some the answer is to immerse themselves in a continual round of parties, music, and fleeting "relationships" (nobody "falls in love" anymore). Life hurts. Things are going terribly wrong. Something must be done to take away the pain. If you were going to the dentist, would you refuse the novocaine? What sense does it make to "just say no" if what is offered seems to be the only way of taking away the hurt?

Others are driven into darkness; more and more young people are practicing demonic rites, hoping to find some measure of power over their circumstances. Now that the good seems hopeless, they turn to ancient evil. Satanism is the number one problem in many high schools in America today.

2. Withdrawal (Introversion). Another way of trying to handle problems in the West is to back out of everything. Pull out of the situation; create another little fantasy world where everything is neat and dreams are already true. Build a castle in the air, then try to move into it. This is the "Jonathan Livingston Seagull" answer. Fly through the rock, and you'll find it is not real; things are not the way they seem. Housewives get addicted to soap operas. Kids lose themselves in a musician, a rock star, adventure gaming. But a Christian Science approach to sin and misery always falls through in the Church. Hurt and sin and death are real. They do not have to be welcomed, but they cannot be ignored.

Joseph could have said, "I don't believe this is happening to me. It is not real at all. I'm not really on a slave caravan. I *can't* be! I'm supposed to have everyone bow down to me, not bow down to everyone else. I refuse to believe it. It is an awful nightmare. I'll wake up one day and I'll be safe in my nice little bed at home."

After a while, those who withdraw begin to go insane. They cannot confront the reality of what is happening. They don't accept the reality in a faith-filled way and say, "This is rotten, but I believe God anyway." It is trust in God that gives us the courage to deal with the hurts of life, because we know that ultimately He is just in all His ways and righteous in all His works, and no matter what comes down, He keeps His promises. The Christian is to be both a realist and an idealist. "He can be," said Peter Marshall, "he must be both."

Even clear, logical thinking that is based on false premises is destructive. Our world has tried to live out assumptions that are lies, and the results are all around us. When smart people see the results of their situations, when smart people try to face pressures in life they were never designed to handle on their own, they break down fast. The less quickly they see it, the slower it takes, but break down they will. That's why some men who originate destructive philosophies go crazy immediately. Those who follow them may not see the consequences as quickly (and sometimes it takes more than a generation to see those consequences), but when they do they all go crazy, too—at once. Bad things *do* happen to good people. Perhaps some terrible wrong happened to you, too, and it is just as bad if not worse than it seems. You can, of course, simply refuse to think about it, to ignore what happened, to try to put it out of your mind. But if you don't face it, you will go crazy.

I was in a city in southern California called La Puente and met a young lady after a meeting there. She said, "There's nothing real in the world. Only what you think is real." I said, "What are you saying?" She said, "For instance, what do you think that is?" She pointed to a piano. I said, "That's a piano." She said, "No, it isn't. It's a blue giraffe." I went over and played a few notes on the blue giraffe and said, "It sure sounds like a piano to me." She said, "You *think* it's a piano because you've chosen to believe it is a piano. But I believe it's a blue giraffe."

She was running away from reality. A girl who has totally blown the moral values of her life and she's trying to say, "This has not happened to me. It's only happened in my mind."

I asked her, "Are you saying there is no external reality other than yourself?" She said, "Yes, the whole world is what you make it."

(John Lennon once wrote a song called "Mind Games." That's what everyone is playing.)

I said, "You're saying nothing is real? Everything you experience is just the projection of your own consciousness?"

"Yes," she said, "that's it exactly. There is nothing real other than what we choose to believe in."

I pulled a Francis Schaeffer trick: I grabbed a pot of hot coffee and held it over her head. She said, "What are you doing?" I said, "I'm just going to pour this pot of hot coffee over your head. But you don't have to worry. If you don't *think* it's there, it won't burn you. I happen to believe it will."

Then I said, "Let's go up on top of this church and jump into the swimming pool." She said, "What swimming pool?" I said, "The one you can believe in on the way down."

Finally, I grabbed her nose. A nose is such a tangible thing. She yelled, "Let go of my nose!" I said, "I don't *have* your nose. You just *think* I have your nose."

Jesus calls us to confront the reality of our situation. He says, "It has happened. It is awful. You have to face it." When the problem is rooted in something we have done wrong we can come to Him and be cleansed, healed, and forgiven. When it is rooted in something others have done, we must forgive and release them from our temptation to bear grudges, hatred, bitterness. The way of denial, of withdrawal, is the way of madness. God calls us to face what has happened honestly, and to use it to throw ourselves more on His love and care.

3. Fatalism (Resignation). The third wrong way to cope with a loss of your dreams is the Eastern way, the way of acceptance. "Whatever is must be." It is *fate, kismet, karma.* Events are but the playing out of a movie; there are sad parts in with the good parts, but it is all at heart just illusion. People don't *have* dreams; they *are* dreams. There are no ultimate absolutes in the universe, and thus no opposites; no good and evil, no right and wrong, no life and death. The world is a *Tao;* reality is where darkness and light are one. God is good/evil, male/female, life/death, and reincarnation will recur until we merge into the Absolute. Everything we experience here is only a dream anyway.

"The truly wise man," said the Maharishi in his commentary on the Bhagavad Gita, "will never weep." Who cares about wars, disasters, destruction, murder? More than 1,700 years ago the Eastern philosopher Plotinus who recorded the ideas of Ammonius Sacchus, founder of the school of Neo-Platonism, put it like this:

> Still more what does it matter when people are devoured [by death] only to return in some new form? It comes to no more than the murder of one of the persons in a play; the actor alters his makeup and returns in a new role. . . . All human intentions are but play, that death is nothing terrible, that to die . . . is to taste a little beforehand what old age has in store, to go away earlier and come back sooner. Murders, death in all its guises . . . all must be to us but the varied incident of a plot, costume on and off, acted grief and lament.

Many people in the West also adopt this attitude, popularized by the New Age movement and spokespeople like Shirley MacLaine whose best-selling books are at heart twentieth-century updates of old and dark Eastern philosophies. Few in the West know what it is like to live in a culture dominated by such darkness; the human sacrifice, the burning of widows in suttee, the caste systems rarely spoken of in polite society in modern India. If all events are necessitated, if everything that happens in life is but the unreeling of film already recorded in the can, then accept we must, and resign ourselves we shall.

The old songs underlined it to previous generations. In the '50s Doris Day sang "Que Sera, Sera"—"Whatever will be, will be." The country-and-western singer of the '60s drawled "Born to Lose," and Steppenwolf in the '70s gave the Hell's Angels an anthem with "Born to Be Wild."

But the way of Christ is never passive acceptance of evil. It is not to admit its necessity or to resign ourselves to the belief that somehow we must learn to coexist with it. Jesus *hated* death, disease, and the rule of the demonic world in people's lives. He healed sicknesses, restored crippled limbs, opened blind eyes and deaf ears. He freed every demonized person He confronted. He never preached a funeral sermon. Instead He broke funerals by the simple expedient of raising the corpse from the dead and restoring the person to his family. Death, like sin and disease, is an enemy in the Bible (1 Corinthians 15:26). The shortest verse in the Bible describes Jesus' own response to the grief, death, and devastation in His poor, broken world: *"Jesus wept"* (John 11:35).

4. A Religious Answer. A fourth option of our time is that of the hurting religious person faced with the collapse of his dreams and the apparent failure of God's promises: It is to *blame God.* To call Him the devil in disguise; to distill all frustration into bitterness, hatred, and resentment and to unload it all on heaven.

That is the trouble with religious idealism when it becomes disillusioned: It quickly turns into radicalism. That's why Marxism could be properly called a Christian heresy. When people with religious backgrounds go sour, they can become the most dangerous people in the world. If our trust in God is inadequate, if we have given ourselves over to religious fantasy that is not founded on biblical revelation and spiritual reality, if we have followed a Christ of our own creation, we will be devastated when it dissolves. *If we have made up an imaginary God we will have to put up with the consequences of an imaginary salvation.* And when such religious idealisms collapse, "great is the fall thereof."

The hardest, most bitter people I have ever met are ex-church people who have turned sour. I can't think of a single atheist I have met in the Western world who has not first had some kind of church background. Most of the really dangerous radicals of our time are people who have given themselves to a religious cause that has been turned significantly to darkness. They become hostile, suspicious, mean. They love no one and expect no love from others. They trust no one and expect no trust from others. This bitterness toward God creates a callous attitude, a cold heart, and hatred not only of God and others, but even of themselves.

The religious person's answer to misplaced trust is often to distill all of his or her bitterness and pour it out on God; to say, in effect, "If *this* is the way it is going to be, God, then forget it. If this is what You had in mind by the dreams You gave me, then You are brutal and vicious and cruel. I trusted You, I listened to You, I believed You, and now everything has fallen apart. See if I ever do anything for You again. See if I ever believe You again. I'm against You, God. I will take my stand against You and I'll do my best to serve Your enemies to the limit of my abilities."

Joseph could have done this. He could have formed the "Egyptian Angels Chariot Club" and ridden around beating up people in border towns in the name of freedom. He could have become a hit man for Pharaoh or formed the S.L.A.—the Slavery Liberation Army. He could have planted bombs in Hebrew baby buggies and booby-trapped Israeli camels. He could have put the blame for everything that happened to him squarely back on the Lord and bitterly resigned himself to what was happening in a lifelong grudge against God.

This was the answer of *Jesus Christ Superstar* when the Judas of the '70s hit album and movie asks Jesus the question "What happened to Your dream?" And Rice and Webber have their Jesus answer: "Then I was inspired. Now I'm sad and tired." Their Christ blames God His Father for what is happening to Him. Like Judas, it is not His fault that things turned out the way they have.

Representations of this fantasy Christ come out in controversial movies like *The Last Temptation of Christ*. They are not new, but as old as every lost religious man's desire to shift the blame for what goes wrong in the world back to God.

But Joseph didn't do it. He refused to do any of these four things. He did not go wild. He did not withdraw. He did not resign himself to what had happened. And above all he did not blame God. Joseph knew he had a dream that was given to him *by God*, and circumstances don't alter divine destiny or dreams.

The classic movie *Ben Hur* explores the rift between two very close boyhood friends. Now adults, grown up apart from each other in two different cultures and worlds, Ben Hur refuses to give the names of some of the Jewish zealots to his Roman friend Messalah, and what begins as a touching re-union turns into a bitter confrontation. "You have no choice," says Messalah. "You are either for me or against me." "Then," replies Ben Hur, "I am *against* you."

Intensely hurt and angry, Messalah strikes back at his former friend, resulting in the destruction of his home, the arrest and imprisonment of his mother and sister, and Ben Hur's being sold into slavery. His world has fallen apart and all because he, like any good Jewish prince, has tried to preserve the religious dreams and ideals of his nation in its devotion to God. Beaten, broken, dying of thirst, with everything loved and secure stripped away from him, Judah ben Hur cries out to the God who seems to have forsaken him.

Then, from the first falling shadow of the Stranger who intervenes to give him water despite a centurion's orders to the contrary, to the final moving moments when he stands beneath the cross on which that same Stranger is dying for the sin and hurt of the world, the film is a statement of the faith-fulness of God. There is healing for your hurt, for your be-trayal, for your anger at what life has dealt you. Do not give up on God. *"His voice,"* says Ben Hur, *"took the sword out of my hand."*

If God has given you a dream, nothing can stop that dream from coming true except your own sin. The Bible says, "If God is for us, who can be against us?" (Roman 8:31). If God has given you a dream, no demon in hell, no self-centered sinner, nobody in this world can stop that from coming true *except yourself*. If you don't learn to react the right way to adversity, if you fall into any of these four traps, then you will blow your dream. The only thing that counts is staying on God's side.

Joseph arrives. He's not blaming God, he's not getting mad or bitter. He's not vowing to himself, "If I ever get out of here I'll pay them back for every rotten thing they tried to do to me. I'm going to kill all my brothers one by one."

He thinks instead: "This is really a mess. My brothers have betrayed me, but *God* can keep me. *God* is faithful. *God* is the One who gave me my dream." So he goes to work as best he knows how in Potiphar's household in Egypt, and he does his work as "unto the Lord." And the funny thing that happens is this: The Egyptian is so excited about Joseph's faithfulness that he makes him head of the servants of the household. God gave him a dream that one day he would be a ruler, and though he is a slave, the pattern of the prophecy begins to be fulfilled.

Now if you were he you might say, "Glory to God! God said I would be in charge one day, and here I am." But fortunately (and unfortunately) that isn't the end of the story. God isn't finished with Joseph yet, and neither is temptation. Enter the femme fatale in the plot. Enter the second great test of his life. Enter the prototype of every *Woman in Red* and *Fatal Attraction* to come. Joseph now has to survive the attempted seduction of Mrs. Potiphar.

A Woman Sets Out to Seduce Him

The recent televangelist sexual and financial scandals that have rocked the church world are unique only in that we live in a world where bad or sad news can be passed on almost instantly. It has certainly become hard to sin in secret in our century. Jesus said, "There is nothing hidden which will not be revealed, nor has anything been kept secret but that it should come to light" (Mark 4:22). There was never a time when this could be made more literally true.

Sin in the Church is something both shocking and sad to God and to His children, but something we have always had to deal with from Bible times to our hi-tech century. Seduction is certainly not something new, but not all seduction is sexual. The love of money seduces; the addiction to pleasure seduces; the privilege of power seduces. A Mrs. Potiphar (whether female or male) is always around to waylay someone with a dream from God, and her determination to make the dreamer fall is frightening to behold.

I suppose she has her own reasons, and all of them make sense to her. Joseph is a slave and he is her husband's legal property. "What is his is rightfully mine," she could say to herself. Besides, there is something exciting about the planned seduction of an unspoiled, clean-living man fresh in from the country. He is no risk. He doesn't have herpes or AIDS and would no doubt be flattered that an attractive and sophisticated woman of power and wealth and position like herself would deign to pay any attention to him at all. So she brushes up on some well-thumbed passages from *The Sensuous Egyptian* and makes her opening gambits.

And to her intense frustration and rising fury, Joseph doesn't play along. For a while she probably thinks he is a bit thick and doesn't know what she has in mind. But after many days of doing everything but leap naked from the chandelier onto him she realizes this devastating truth: He isn't interested. Not only does he smile politely and pass by every approach, he even takes to going out of his way not to be found in the house alone with her.

Why *doesn't* Joseph succumb to temptation? He is young, no doubt anxious to please, and probably a bit lonely. He is far from home in a place where no one knows of or cares about his childhood commitment to God. This alluring woman is both willing and able to provide him with what seems to be an even greater level of security and power; in fact, to shun her attractive advances might be downright dangerous. If he looks only at his past disappointments, his present circumstances, and his future situation, surrender to this attractive seduction is a foregone conclusion. If Joseph at that point decides that his childhood dream is out of reach, we all know what the next lines of his story would be.

And all of us have been there, too. Perhaps not every seduction looks like his, but the name of the game is always the same. And perhaps if we had been where Joseph stood, the story would have turned out the way everybody would expect it to.

But it doesn't. Shockingly it doesn't. Joseph does something that seems so strange, so odd, so gauche in a modern world like ours that is without convictions, without absolutes, without ultimate commitments. He says *no.* He turns her down, not because he might get caught, or because he might get hurt, or because she isn't quite his "type." *He turns her down because he doesn't want to hurt God.* He has a dream God has given him to treasure, and he feels that God would never let down someone who loves Him. He trusts God, and rests his case in His hands. He looks to Him to meet his needs. And so he says to the greatest temptation he has ever had in his life, "How can I do this wicked thing and sin against God?"

If you haven't read the story you might expect that things go great from that moment on. Like: "Mrs. Potiphar breaks down and weeps, apologizes to Joseph for the madness that came over her, gets saved and recommits her devotion and marriage to her rightful husband. Then Mr. Potiphar is so impressed that he also gets saved and begins a church in his house attended by many of his soldiers, and pastored of course by Brother Joseph. A great revival eventually sweeps the Egyptian army and leads ultimately to Joseph's being returned to his homeland where his brothers are all so impressed by his achievements they welcome him home. . . ." And so on. . . . (Fade to black, Handel's *Messiah* or perhaps "Chariots of Fire" playing in the background; run "The End.")

But reality is different. What actually follows is even *worse* than before. Mrs. Potiphar, in a mad rage, rips off his clothes. Joseph becomes the world's first "streaker for righteousness." He barely gets out of the house with anatomy intact, let alone his dignity. And then in furious retribution for his deflating and humiliating refusal, to her husband she accuses him of rape. Only his previous knowledge of both his wife and his captured Hebrew slave's character (and perhaps the intervention of God) stops Potiphar short of killing Joseph on the spot. But it's into a dungeon for Joseph the dreamer, Joseph the man of God, Joseph the faithful. And *where is his marvelous dream now?*

From slavery to a prison? That's *down*, not up! Things are looking darker than ever for Joseph. Honestly now, would you have thrown in the towel? Would you? *Did* you? After being slung into a filthy hole seemingly to rot away for life, would you say, "O.K. That's it. I've about had it with this righteousness stuff. God, why in the world would You let her do that? Why couldn't You just have moved me on somewhere else where I would have at least had a chance?"

But Joseph is incorrigibly, embarrassingly *faithful*. (Some people never learn.) He says, "Glory to God anyway. I still have a dream." And he goes to work in the prison until he is made ruler of the prison. The most important thing we can notice right here is this: "But *the Lord was with Joseph* and showed him mercy, and He gave him favor. . . . Because the Lord was with him; and whatever he did, the Lord made it prosper" (Genesis 39:21, 23, emphasis added).

One day Pharaoh has a big tiff with his butler and his baker. They are unable to shred the evidence in time and both end up in prison under the care and friendship of Joseph. And one day they both have dreams. The butler says, "I had a big bunch of grapes on three branches and I squeezed out some wine for Pharaoh and he drank it. I wonder what in the world that means?"

Joseph is an expert on dreams by now; he's had one himself a long time that has never been fulfilled. In fact, he has thought about it every which way for years and is real sensitive spiritually whenever someone mentions "dreams." He says, "I know what your dream means. In three days you are going to be restored as Pharaoh's butler. Just one thing," he adds sadly. "When it happens (and it will happen) will you put in a good word for me with Pharaoh?"

The baker is encouraged no end by this interpretation of the butler's dream, so he shares his dream with Joseph, too. Unfortunately, not all dream interpretations turn out to be positive. Just as Joseph discerns, Pharaoh restores the butler but executes the baker. And the one last request that Joseph makes to the butler as he leaves the prison, "Remember me," is wiped away in the relief of his release.

A Friend Forgets Him

There is something even worse than being betrayed or tempted and that is to be *forgotten*. Many a man or woman of God with a dream has made it gloriously first through hurt and even through various attempts at seduction, only to lose the race at last with the finishing tape in sight, to fall to the creeping despair of being apparently ignored, shelved, consigned to oblivion. In betrayal you at least have something significant enough for others to be threatened; in seduction you have something important enough to be the target of temptation. But in oblivion you stand to lose everything that ever made you or your dream worthwhile. And Joseph has to face it, just as you or anyone else who has been given a dream by God will have to face it. What do you do if after all your faithfulness, everyone, even those you counted on as friends, *just forget you?*

Being forgotten: to go out with neither a bang nor even a whimper but only an emptiness; to have wanted to make some kind of splash in the lily pond of life but leaving not even a ripple, nothing more than the effect on the water an hour after you pull out your hand. "The central neurosis of our time," said a famous psychiatrist, "is emptiness." It is the ultimate terror; it is the final level at which faith is tried to see if it may be found finally true.

Days go by, weeks, months for Joseph as he waits in vain for a word from the grateful butler, but still no message comes. And as the months stretch out into a whole year, then another, it seems as if Job's wife had the final insight into the real running of the world: "Do you still hold to your integrity? Curse God and die!" (Job 2:9).

But Joseph does not. Doggedly, faithfully, determined to trust God to the day he dies, he goes on with his tasks, running the prison, loving God, serving to the best of his ability. Good old Joseph is still good old *ingenuous* Joseph. He hasn't become cynical Joseph, now-I-know-better, once-bitten-twice-shy Joseph muttering to himself as he clenches his teeth, "I've been umpteen years in this rotten place. Where is God when you need Him?" And the God who never forgets, who in absolute justice and absolute goodness rules the universe, is not finished writing this story yet.

The genius of the ingenuous one is his ability to work with reversals of the plan. And God is the greatest genius in the universe. He rules over what jealous, sneaky, or nasty people are up to. He takes the intentions of the wicked and weaves their ugly purposes into scenarios that one day proclaim to all watching worlds His greatness and His glory. God delights in overthrowing the evil schemes of men and devils and fulfilling exactly what He says He is going to do.

If God makes you a promise, you are going to see that promise come true. Who cares *who* says it "cannot," "will not" happen? If He says it will, it will. If He has to move heaven and earth to do it, He will fulfill His Word. He has magnified His Word above His name, and His name is Faithful and True, the God who cannot lie.

Joseph is in jail. The world is quiet, and Pharaoh has a dream. It terrifies him. It bothers him intensely. It is only a dream about cows, seven fat cows and seven skinny cows. And right on its heels another one, starring fat ears of corn and skinny ears of corn. The seven dream cows with anorexia take out the seven plump ones. The seven wind-blasted ears of corn cannibalize the seven Kellogg's pin-up ears. And Pharaoh hasn't got a clue as to what this deeply disturbing set of night revelations means.

"Pour me some of that wine, butler," he says. "I just had a dream that scared the living incense out of me. I know it's important, and I know it has something to do with the nation, but every charlatan I know has referred me to crystals, cards, and animal entrails and I'm not getting any joy from them at all. And you know what I do when I'm not happy with my staff. . . ."

The butler's hand shakes a little as he pours the wine. "So what do you think, butler? And don't talk to me about pyramid power. I built them myself and I know that's not going to show me what I need to know. If there were only someone trustworthy in the kingdom, someone who wouldn't want to use me or rip me off, *someone* who could tell me what these dreams mean. . . ."

And the butler says: "Uh-oh."

Pharaoh is the king of the known world, and God deals with him directly. You may not think about God much when you are busy running the world. You may not plan to fit Him into your schedule. You can fill your waking hours with business, pleasure, and everything else you can imagine to shut out His voice, but you can't get away from Him if He is going to deal with you.

The butler remembers. "There was this guy. Name of Joseph. He told me about my dream. Right on, he was. Never saw a man before or since who knew more about dreams."

"Where is he?"

"Prison, last time I knew."

"Prison! Get him out and bring him here."

And in minutes, pausing only for a shave and change of

clothes, Joseph goes from prison to the presence of the Pharaoh of the world.

"I know what your dream means," says Joseph. "There are coming seven years of plenty to this country and then seven years of famine. God has spoken twice to the Pharaoh and that means it's not only sure, it will happen soon. What you should do is appoint someone really wise and trustworthy to supervise storage during the plenty years for the coming famine. That's my advice to Pharaoh."

"That's incredible!" says the Pharaoh. "I can't find anyone in my kingdom made as smart and trustworthy by God as you. You're elected. You're my number one man."

Boom. From prison to number two in the world in an hour. That's what God does.

For seven years Joseph supervises food and stores grain and then the predicted famine comes. Joseph's family runs out of food and only Egypt has grain to sell. At Jacob's bidding, his sons make the long and risky journey to Egypt to seek the favor of this new ruler under Pharaoh. To get grain you have to go through him. If he cuts you off, you die. Everything depends on their making the right impression, as they are ushered into the audience of the awful presence that sits beside the throne of Egypt.

And then you know what happens. The brothers file humbly in, totally unaware of who it is they are bowing down before. Joseph is looking at them, and it is all he can do to stop himself from crying. He is thinking, *Glory to God. Glory to God.* He listens to them protesting for their lives and for their little brother's life and for their old dad Jacob back home waiting and praying the ruler of Egypt will show mercy to their family. Joseph is thinking about what his little brother looks like now, and what his dad looks like now, and finally he can't stand it. They are all sitting there whispering desperately to each other in Hebrew, not knowing Joseph understands, not knowing who he is, conscious only that they are at the total mercy of a man who could snap his fingers like that and have them all annihilated.

He tells them they must return again for food and bring with them their little brother Benjamin or be cut off from provision and die. How Joseph manages to go that long without revealing his secret I'll never know. But the time comes when he stands up before them, clears the court, and faces them all alone. Choking back the tears he asks them, "Do you know who I am?" His brothers look at him. They still feel the guilt of long, long ago. They are scared. They are worried. They *don't* know who he is. He's the second ruler in the world, isn't he? What does he mean?

"*I am Joseph.*"

The dream. The dream comes true. Literally, in a way not even Joseph in his wildest child's imagination could have guessed, the God who gave him his dream fulfills it to the uttermost. And Joseph, unable to restrain the sobs, has the happiest moment of his life. It is God, wholly God, *God* who has worked with him all along. The betrayals, temptations, burials of the past are forgotten; nothing he has been through matters anymore. "God sent me before you to preserve a posterity for you in the earth, and to save your lives by a great deliverance. So now it was not you who sent me here, but God; and He has made me a father to Pharaoh, and lord of all his house, and a ruler throughout all the land of Egypt" (Genesis 45:7–8).

Nothing can stop a God-given dream. If you drop it, someone else will pick it up and run in your place. God will do what He has promised; but great dreams mean great trials and great responsibilities. And if you have a dream given you by God, you, too, are going to have to learn how to deal with the pressures set against that dream.

What to Do When Your Dreams Seem to Destruct

First, face honestly what happened. It may have been sin, it may have been yours, it may have been another's, but the

damage has been done. If you have lost something precious
tell the Lord: "It's gone and it will never come back. That's it.
But Lord, You gave me a dream and somehow despite everything, despite my own weakness and inability and failure, You
can find a way to glorify Yourself and fulfill Your promises."

Second, next time you must absolutely refuse to get bitter.
You have no cause to blame God, and you must steadfastly
refuse to harbor bitterness or grudges against those who have
done you real or imagined wrong. If you harbor hurt, your
prayers will only hit the ceiling. You *must* forgive. John Wesley met a man who said, "Sir, I never forgive." John Wesley
said, "Then, sir, I hope you never sin." Unforgiveness is not
an option in relation to a dream sent from God.

**Third, you are going to have to use your present circum-
stances creatively.** Use what problems you now face to practice your dream. So God called you to the mission field. But
here you are stuck in some little Podunk place that doesn't
look or sound like any mission field you ever imagined. Practice all you have in Podunk. Give Podunk your best shot.
Don't get a vision for all of Africa until you have begun out of
a full heart to evangelize your own "Pumpkin Holler." Serve
where you are now in Jesus' name and gladly for His sake.
The only thing you want to be *sure* of is that "God is with
you." Learn to do what God calls you to do even in the
limiting circumstances you may feel "in prison" with.

The late Peter Marshall, Sr., had a beautiful parable on an
oyster. It is just lying there, innocent, opening its little shell
and sucking in seawater to keep itself alive and a piece of grit
lands right in its tender gut. Now faced with such a problem
our oyster might say (if oysters could talk or think like us and
with apologies to Peter Marshall),"There is no grit in my gut.
I do not believe this. I will turn out from my saline consciousness any thought of grit."

Or he could say, "Why did God send me this grit? What did

I do to deserve grit? God, I can't believe You would do a painful thing like this to a faithful oyster like me."

Or he could just say, "Get me a stiff drink of seaweed. I'm hurting and it's not going away. I'm going to get thoroughly wasted and forget my pain."

Or he might say, "Well, that's the way it is with us oysters. *Que será, será.* It comes. It goes."

But the oyster doesn't say any of those things. The oyster, as Marshall said, is a "realist as well as an idealist." The oyster knows it has a problem that will not go away so it does something about it. It begins to coat that grit with a milky substance that it produces until finally it winds up with a pearl—in Peter Marshall's words, "A thing of beauty wrapped around trouble." And that's the way God makes His pearls.

Starting with problems that sinful people or the demonic world puts into your life, God turns them through your godly response by His grace into great treasure; He makes them ultimately into something precious and beautiful. Loren Cunningham says, "God delights in taking lemons and making them into lemonade." It doesn't ultimately matter what happens to you *as* a Christian as long as you truly *are* a Christian, a child of God, in love with God to the end. God can and will fulfill His dreams in you. The dream goes on and you can be there to see it.

Prayer

Lord Jesus, You are the One who went before us to taste the sting of both life and death for every man and woman in our world. We thank You we can speak with You as a man speaks face to face with a friend; for You Yourself became a man and lived among us and You know perfectly what it is to be human.

You know what it is to be brought before enemies and to have them mock You; to be with close friends and still not have them understand You. You know what it is like to be misrepresented and misunderstood; You know what it means to be despised and rejected, to be humiliated and hated, to cry real tears, and to know loneliness and grief and sorrow. Though You were God's own Son, You did not count equality something to be grasped after; You laid aside Your own rights in order to win the right for us to enter in at the throne of the Father in heaven.

Because You cared enough to die for us, we can ask in turn for ourselves to die to all self-seeking ambition; and because You live, we shall live also. Give us the courage to walk on from the dust of our past with all its failures and loss; to walk with our heads held high because of Your help and Your love;

to walk on with dignity as Your forgiven children without turning aside from this road You have already traveled on our behalf. We love You, Lord, and we believe; help Thou our unbelief.

Level Three

Water to the Loins

"Unless I see, I will not believe."
—Thomas to the disciples

"Again he measured a thousand and led me through the water, water reaching the loins."   Ezekiel 47:4, NAS

4

The Challenge to Your Emotional Levels

When you hear the Ezekiel phrase *waters to the loins* in a sermon, some preachers will refer to the river's "touching your pockets" and the necessity of giving. Actually there are probably more primary meanings. Robes didn't have pockets in Bible times.

What do the loins signify in Scripture? These things: (1) the focus of power of your life, or your strength; (2) security; (3) the reproductive side of your life, or your creativity; and (4) the vulnerability and sensitivity of your life.

Strength

I asked a friend who is a legendary pro tennis player what physically goes first in competitive tennis. She said, "Your stomach." I said, "What do you mean, your stomach?" I would have thought your legs, your arms—perhaps as you get older and are still running around in the heat, even your brains— but no, her answer was your stomach. And a year later, playing for hours in a grueling tennis match, I suddenly found out what she meant. My arms were still there. My legs would still move. I still knew what I was supposed to be doing. The only trouble was, something in the very center of my body just quit.

You've probably noticed how weight lifters wear those wide belts. Why do they wear them? Here is one reason: If they sneeze at the wrong time, perhaps while power-lifting some megaweight, their bodies could give out there at its weakest spot. All the focus of our strength flows right through here.

The most vulnerable area of your body is the loins. That's why the Roman belt alluded to in the armor of God mentioned in Ephesians 6:14 was no little Gucci designer creation. It was a big, strong, broad belt. It was more than a support, something to hold up your toga; it was also a protective device. For the loins also represent your security.

Security

What are you really resting on? In what is your final confidence? Where is the ultimate base of your security? As we grow in grace, we learn some things in our walks with God that become life-messages to us, the central descriptions of our purpose in the world. We have some things that we consider very strong in our lives; they become areas we consider places of power, the focus of our God-given abilities.

And therein lies a danger. Our strengths can betray us. We can shift our reliance in subtle ways from trust in God, who gifts us, to trust in His gifts. We can lean on what He gave us and forget the Giver. But when the river rises to the loins, for the first time we realize that we are reaching a place where we can no longer dictate the situation.

Jesus is the only One I know who can look you in the eye, tell you how you are going to die, smile, and say, "Follow Me." He said it to Peter. "When you were younger," He told him, "you girded yourself and walked where you wished; but when you are old . . . another will gird you and carry you where you do not wish" (John 21:18).

There may come a time to you, too, when everything you could once do easily is threatened by the river; it moves to the place of your security and promises to carry you where you never intended to go.

The truth is we can't find ultimate security in any man-made institution. So much that we have relied on recently in the Church has dramatically failed us. We have looked up to and trusted people and they have failed, looked up to and trusted ministries and they have failed, relied on tried-and-trusted methods and approaches and formulae and, unaccountably, they, too, have failed. Our media are full of these failures in the Church; every day seems to bring a new exposé of people who have blown it one way or another in morals, in finances, in misused authority. The world is filled with hurt people who have trusted in someone or something that has gone badly astray.

Creativity

Another major area represented by the loins is, of course, the reproductive center of our lives; it is the focus of our sexuality, our ability to procreate, and thus the source of our initiating new life. And it is also in the area of our creativity that the waters will reach us, threatening all that we have been good at making and initiating and bringing into being. There may come a time when everything you have done well in now fails. You were once a wellspring of creativity; now, unaccountably, the spring seems to have failed. You were the one who had all the ideas; now they are gone. Our strengths are often the sources of our greatest weaknesses so God must also search us out here. What we have relied on outside of God Himself to carry us must fail, in order that we may learn again what it is to trust solely in Him.

Sensitivity

You may have noticed that writers in the King James Version of the Bible sometimes used the word *bowels* to refer to our affection, our compassion, the innermost being and emotional depths of our lives. (See Genesis 43:30; 1 Kings 3:26; Isaiah 63:15; Jeremiah 31:20; Philippians 1:7;1 John 3:17; etc.)

Here, too, the waters to the loins touch us. It is not until water gets to your waist that you really notice how *cold* it is. In almost every culture on earth, covering is placed around the loins. To be stripped naked is not merely something physical. It is also mental and emotional and spiritual, tied in since the fall of Adam and Eve (who once were "naked and not ashamed") with the whole core of our self-protection, self-image, and self-preservation. To be stripped naked is so fundamental a shame that it is given as a judgment in Scripture, one that touches us in the very deepest levels of our being. And when Jesus the Lord was hung on the cross, He was stripped naked Himself for our sakes. He was raked to the very depths for the covered-over secret sins of His fallen world.

Living in the communication-rich Western world has its unique advantages and its hidden consequences. We are continually exposed to the constant clamor of sophisticated media. It can result in what we could call "emotional shell-shock."

Faced with a constant barrage of demanding, exciting, scary, sad, painful, and frightening images, we learn in a way to live like someone in a war. If we have a choice, we get ourselves out of the danger, we switch off or disconnect the source. If we don't, we try to somehow dull out our responses; we steel ourselves to what is going on, and try to ignore our feelings. A person who has been badly shaken in combat one too many times goes over the edge into the rigid irresponsiveness we call "shell-shock."

A similar thing can happen to us right in our living rooms. Every day we can see hundreds of sophisticated commercials demanding our attention. We turn on the news; there are the headlines deemed currently significant, footage of new tragedies, of crimes or wars, brilliantly edited and presented as impending threats to our health, our family, or the entire planet. For entertainment we can watch close-ups of our favorite sports stars in the "thrill of victory" or the "agony of defeat," or see some multi-million-dollar dramatization, calculated by a team of talented professionals to make us laugh or cry or scare the living daylights out of us.

All these are vicarious; we are not really there and we rarely if ever share in the events we see. So we get to feel the feeling without actually having the experience. We experience reality secondhand. And the effect over a period of time is this: Either we learn to tune out deep emotions in self-defense or we need deeper and deeper levels of manufactured emotion to move us.

That's one of the reasons many modern kids like gory and scary horror movies. They have been exposed constantly to hurt and fear and shock. It takes something quite drastic now to move them. And drastic provision there is. Rock stars compete with ear-bleeding sound systems, outlandish stage acts, and more violent, mind-blowing, and extravagant sets. Music videos have to be full of drama, shock, and weirdness; metal singers have to scream for attention. There's a lot of competition for an audience out there and the ones who are noticed (any way they can be) are the ones who make the charts and the bucks. Listen to media-saturated kids today and you'll hear it. Their most common complaint and comment is this: "Boring, it's so-o-o boring." Emotional shell-shock. Either we turn it off (limit the input) or learn to turn ourselves off and limit our responses.

And this, too, has affected the Church in the West. We are not deeply moved by much. We have learned to carry our filters and screens and reservations around with us, to protect our deep levels of feeling from anything that may affect us profoundly. In consequence, we are often emotionally and in other ways shallow. We feel few things deeply. We are sheltered, secure, protected. We carry our defenses against mediated, secondhand feelings into the sanctuary and even into the inner court of God. We will not be affected, even by real events that demand real feelings. We are never caught naked and we are never ashamed. But that must change if we want to be serious with God. The river is rising. It is reaching for the depths of our emotions, and we will experience again reality firsthand.

Now it is in this area that we come to a major thing God is doing in the Church. There is unexpected danger in the comfort of inner strength, security, creativity, sensitivity. That danger is that we know the principle so well, we know the law, the rules, the tradition that have given us shelter so well, that we become entranced with the shelter and not with the Person who gave it.

God has a remedy for that. The water moves "up to the loins." We need something in our lives to threaten profoundly all our reliance on even the good things, the right, true, and proven things, the things we have learned to trust that have nevertheless moved us away from trust in God alone. We need to be stripped in a deep way. And this is where a whole new struggle begins.

5

Our Struggle with Doubt

Although everyone has experienced it, few people today have thought deeply about doubt. It is one of the most misunderstood problems in life. We always tend automatically to equate doubt with unbelief. It is not the same thing at all!

One of the few contemporary books on this theme was done by Os Guinness, a friend, teacher, and author who is an articulate and well-informed spokesman for the cause of Christ and for a biblical world view. I was first privileged to meet Os some years ago when he was teaching with Francis and Edith Schaeffer at L'Abri in Switzerland. I have always found his work both challenging and stimulating. Os put together one of the best overviews in print on the subject of doubt, one that certainly deserves more exposure. His book *In Two Minds* is a major source for much of what I have recast in simpler form here and is must reading for people who want to explore this area in more detail.

Os first of all defines doubt scripturally. Here are his five Bible words for doubt, and the first one is very easy to remember. It's in James 1:6 and it is "Don't waver." "He who doubts is like a wave of the sea driven and tossed by the wind." The Greek word is *dipsukos*, which means "to be chronically double-minded." A double-minded man is "unstable in all his ways" (James 1:8).

Next there is *diakrino.* It means "to discern," and is a stronger form of the verbs *to sunder* or *to separate.* It means that you are so torn between two options that you cannot make up your mind. It's used, for instance, in Mark 11:23: "Whoever says to this mountain, 'Be removed and be cast into the sea,' and does not doubt in his heart. . . ." (See also Matthew 21:21; Acts 10:20, 11:12; Romans 4:20, 14:23.)

There is a restaurant in northern California near Sabastapol where I used to live. It serves only three things: great steak, fish, and chicken. And the waitresses, I think, are trained to make a point of being rude to the customers about it. You see "Steak, Fish, Chicken" painted on the wall when you come in and sit down. There's no menu and you say, "Is there a menu?" "No," says the waitress, hand on her hip, "we don't *have* menus. Can't you read? Fish, steak, chicken. That's it! So *whaddya want?*" So before she really gets tough and punches me out, I say (in true character): "I'll take the chicken."

You know the good thing about a small menu? It makes it easier to decide. It's the multiple options of our society that have given people this looseness, this being in two minds, this being torn between this and that. That's one of the Bible words for doubt, *diakrino.*

A third word for doubt is the word from which we get the word *meteor, meteorizomi.* The word means "to raise up or suspend or to soar or lift oneself up." This idea is to be arrogant or proud. But another meaning, the way it's used in the Bible for doubt, is to be "hung up." We use that in the vernacular—to be "hung up," to be "up in the air" about something. That's what a meteor is—up in the air. To be hung up, to be unsettled, to be tense, doubtful. We also call it ambivalence. This is the word used in Luke 12:29: Jesus said, "Don't worry—don't be hung up—about these things." Don't be hung up about food and dress and where we're living. . . .

A fourth word for doubt is the word we get *dialogue* from, *dialogizomai*. The word means "thought" or "inner debate." "Should I do it? Should I not do it?" Talking to yourself. Dialogue. In Luke 24:38 Jesus said: "Why are you troubled?" In other words, "Why do questions arise in your mind? Why are you having this inner debate?" (See also Matthew 16:19; Luke 2:35, 5:22, 6:8, 9:46–47; Romans 1:21, 14:1; 1 Corinthians 3:20; Philippians 2:14; 1 Timothy 2:8.)

The last word, *distasia*, is found in Matthew 14:31. We get an account of the disciples who are out in the sea. A big storm comes up and threatens to sink the boat. They're scared out of their minds. Jesus is off somewhere on His own being spiritual, praying, and they're all going to drown. They just don't know what to do.

In the middle of it, here comes Jesus. He has no ground or sea transport available, so He just walks right across the sea toward the boat! Peter looks at this white apparition coming toward him, perhaps flapping in the howling wind and waves, and he is totally terrified. *There's something coming toward the boat walking on the water!* They are not only going to die; first they are going to be attacked by a ghost. All the disciples hide behind Peter. Then through the roar of the storm and the waves, in the licking of the lightning they hear these words: "Don't be afraid! It is I."

I know what Peter's thinking: "*Who* is I?" It *sounds* like the Lord. But most normal people don't walk on water, especially in the middle of a storm. So Peter the disciple with the foot-shaped mouth does it again. He says, "If that's really You, bid me come to You the way You are coming to us."

There's this pregnant silence. Then Peter hears what he probably never expected or wanted to hear: "Come."

Peter puts one foot out, then both feet. He even gets to take a few steps into miracle and mystery before remembering a lecture he heard at the University of Babylon on "Relative Density" and he goes under. A hand reaches down and grabs him and here's what Jesus says: "You of little faith. Why did you doubt?"

The word is *hesitate*, to hold back. "Why didn't you just keep coming?" It is the same word that is used in Matthew 28:17 when Jesus rose from the dead and they saw Him and they worshiped, "but some doubted." They held back.

If we put all of these five words together, we come up with what the word *doubt* really means. It is not the same as unbelief. Unbelief is "I don't care what God says; I'm not going to do it." Unbelief is a refusal to commit yourself to something seen quite clearly as true. Faith is "I see it and I'm going to do it." Doubt is "I am in two minds about it. I don't know what to do. I'm up in the air about it. I'm hesitating. I'm not sure." Doubt, says Os Guinness, is always a halfway house. There is no such thing as "total doubt." Doubt is always in between.

Actually, doubt is not the opposite of faith. When you doubt, it is not some cowardly betrayal of Jesus and a surrender to the wrong side.

The relationship between doubt and faith is more like the relationship between courage and fear. The opposite of courage is cowardice, not fear. Here's a person in a war who, though he's afraid, lets courage master his fear and goes ahead and does it anyway. Or take climbing a mountain. Healthy fear can be a good thing as long as it does not rule you in the hard or dangerous parts of the climb. So, likewise, faith doesn't mean that you will have no doubt. It just means that one overrules the other.

Doubt is never to be encouraged, of course, just as fear is not something given by God. Doubt is a transitional situation, something to be passed through and passed on. You can trust God in the middle of doubt just as you can be brave in the midst of fear. You come down on the side of what God says and you go on anyway. Like Peter, you put your foot down on the water despite everything that threatens you and you walk toward Jesus. Peter in the storm wasn't walking on the water.

He was walking on a *word*, and the word was from the One who made water, and the word was "Come."

Why does doubt devastate us so deeply? Because the bottom line of everything in life is trust. Without faith, it is impossible to please God (Hebrews 11:6). And when trust is threatened, betrayed, or put on the line, the wound is always huge because trust is the basis for everything between people. In every relationship—family, marriage, home, business, devotions, friendships—trust is the foundation.

God is a Person. Because we are made in His image, we are designed to draw our ultimate sense of personhood from Him. From His personality, we get the idea of our own sense of personality. To know God is to trust Him. To trust Him, then, is also to know ourselves better. That's why if we get our eyes off God we always have problems finding out who we really are.

The spirit of the world blatantly reverses that order. It says, "Express yourself!" or "Be yourself!" as if you were in real danger of becoming a carrot or something. But Jesus says, "Deny yourself." Try to find your value in other people, even in close relatives, and you will always be a loser. But give your life away to your Creator and you will discover why you were born. In other words, "He who finds his life will lose it, and he who loses his life for My sake will find it" (Matthew 10:39). And only an infinite God, expressing Himself in finite beings, can give us infinite diversity. None of us will ever be boringly alike unless we take our eyes off Christ as our prime focus and try to start cloning our visions and goals and character from each other. God's call to us is just: "Love Me. Don't try to be like anyone else. Just forget yourself and love Me." And in that uniqueness formed of trust, the closer you get to God, the more different you become from anybody else.

The more *un*like God you are, the more like the same mud of unsaved humanity you are. If you meet one drug addict, you've met them all. Meet one liar, you've met the prototype of all liars at all times. There are no new sins; there are no new, "creative" ways of wrongdoing. And the same is true in self-expression. Try to emphasize your own uniqueness, focus on "being yourself," and you usually wind up just like everyone else. Isn't it sad to see little kids all dressed up like Madonna or Rambo so they can be really different? That is why the "chief end of man" is to "glorify God and enjoy Him forever." That is why doubt is so devastating to us—because it attacks not only our trust, it attacks ourselves. It destroys our own ideas of what personhood is. Doubt is intimately linked with the matter of trust and trustworthiness.

To understand and react correctly to doubt will help equip us for two things. First, there is going to be a *radical apostasy* in the last days. (See 2 Timothy 3:1–5; 2 Peter 2:1–3, 12–22.) We know that. You have probably seen it. How many times do you hear, "I was once a Christian"? It is devastating in the West, where many people have given up their so-called "faith in Christ," or at least some professed form of Christianity. A lot of this defection, of course, stems from never really having come to grips with true Christianity; their contact with true faith is only a shallow thing. But some of it has to do with church people's going through some experience of not being able to handle doubt.

Doubt is common in one way or another to every child of God. Doubt comes to us all in different ways. And viewed correctly in the the light of God's purposes for us, doubt can even be a positive factor. Like temptation properly responded to, doubt can bring us into a better place with Christ.

Number two reason for the necessity of a time of doubt is *preparation for the years of testing.* I believe also that we in the West have entered a time of great testing. That decade of pessimism, of malaise and questioning, has already begun. It is not only happening; it is happening faster. Notice how everything is compressing? The consciousness generated by the '60s took about fifteen years; the '70s took about eight; the '80s took about six. We're already in the '90s. This is a time of serious testing, of pressure, of concentrated searching, and, if God's allowance of doubt has not done its work properly, some of us may not survive spiritually.

There is even something good that can come out of a time of pessimism. In good times, people often forget their source of blessings. It is harder to speak to a man who is lost and happy than a man who is lost and hurting. There is a shallow optimism that often rules in people's lives when everything is all right. They tend to take life for granted, not think much about the serious issues of life. But when times are hard, when there are days of darkness, when the bottom drops out of the stock market, when the nations shake and the world moves a step closer to total destruction, people begin to think a lot more. They ask questions, they wonder about their priorities, about what is really important. And while times of doubt are always times of shaking and uncertainty, they can lead to important changes in the way we think and feel and act.

6

Seven Kinds of Doubt

God is out to bring us to what we might call *radical trust*. What does that mean? It means, says Os Guinness, faith plus nothing. Not faith plus a good community of friends. Not faith plus ministry. Not faith plus people whom I can look up to. Not faith plus a lifestyle that happily enough agrees with the particular one I've presently chosen. Just *faith plus nothing*. Trusting in Him, that's it.

Final abandonment involves God's dealing with us even in principles we have trusted in—good principles, even godly principles that we have come nevertheless to rely on other than God Himself. That means that He is going to take all the things that we are so strong in and turn them under His careful hand into nothing. The things we know so well and are so reliable will fall apart. The house will leak. The business will fail. Your best bell-ringing sermon will be met with stony silence. Your joke will bomb, your singing voice will crack in public, your very best friend will blow it. The car, the equipment, the sound system, which has been previously flawless, will die.

Your strength is also your greatest weakness. And this necessary step when the water touches the loins must be death. Here is a summary of what Os Guinness sees as the seven different kinds of families of doubt. For details and much more content, get the book and read it carefully for yourself. Here my only concern is to introduce you to the problem on a very general level and relate it to the peculiar needs of our particular time. The first four levels of doubt have to do with a faulty *premise*, a poor or inadequate understanding of what it really means to be a Christian. This carries right into our Christian lives. The last three levels have to do with failure in the outworking of our Christian lives in *practice*.

Independence and Ingratitude

The first major cause of doubt Os examines has to do with *independence and ingratitude*. That's why we looked in our analogy of the river at the water rising to the knees. The danger of being made truly free in God is that you can move quite subtly from being free *under* God to becoming free *from* God. And in our four-level river analogy it goes like this: First, before it touched your ankles, you were a chaotic person. Now your needs are met and you have become resourceful; you are cleansed, given dignity and responsibility and perhaps even a ministry.

Take a kid, for example, who was a drug addict, in prison all the time, a real cancer in society. He gets saved. He sets his heart on loving God and people. Now he becomes in his own eyes significant. Now he realizes his value. He begins to preach. His ministry meets some needs. Large crowds come out to hear him. Now he's considered somebody important. There are a lot of people looking up to him for help, for answers, for an example. And now his temptation is different from when he was in the streets.

Similarly, when first our needs are met by Christ, we develop under Him some resourcefulness. The problem comes when that God-sufficiency begins to turn into self-sufficiency and, finally, independence. It's an independent spirit that wipes out more people than anything else. Satan didn't get in trouble trying to run off with some lady angel. His ultimate problem was an independent spirit. It's very subtle. No one would ever say, "Hey, I don't need Jesus anymore. I'm going to do this sort of stuff on my own." It never happens like that. It goes like this: We begin to focus on what we do well. We've got it down. And as we magnify in our own hearts how well we can do what we can do, we forget that what we have was given (John 3: 27). God does a slow fade.

What do you think God is really going to do at this stage? It's not something *bad* that is the idol of our lives; it may well be the gifts He has given us that are now becoming gods. How do you deal with the idolatry of a gift *given to you by God?* How do you deal with something given *by* Him that has taken His place? That's the situation of Abraham and Isaac. Isaac was given to Abraham by God (Genesis 18:11–14, 21:1–8). Now for Abraham to take that thing that was not only most precious to him but even given him in a miracle by God, to have to "deliver it to the death," to give it back. . . . It seemed just incredible. Yet God so tested Abraham, and the old warrior came through with flying colors (Genesis 22:15–18).

So here is really the heart of dealing with doubt on this level: "Blessed are the poor in spirit" (Matthew 5:3). Our antidote to ingratitude is many times spoken of in Scripture. It speaks of *"giving thanks"* (Ephesians 5:20), *"not forgetting"* (Deuteronomy 4:9, 6:12, 8:11; Psalm 78:7, 103:2; Jeremiah 2:32), and *"remembering"* (Deuteronomy 8:18; 1 Chronicles 16:12; Psalm 25:6; Ecclesiastes 12:1; Acts 20:35; Revelation 3:3). This is to be a genuine, unforced, and heartfelt response to God's goodness and provision. We can get so mechanical in giving thanks that that is all it is—a form and a tradition. Or we can get so loose over it that we forget. So thankfulness should be like a little bright thread that runs through all kinds of formal and informal occasions of giving thanks and remembrance.

In the Bible, Jesus said in one sad situation: "Were there

not ten lepers healed?" Only one came back to thank Him; the others were so excited about their miracle they forgot the God who made it possible (Luke 17:11–19). It is important that God is remembered and thanked. In Numbers 15:38–39 we read that the Israelites were even supposed to put special threads in their clothes to remind them to give thanks. They remembered God's salvation with unleavened bread (Exodus 13:3–10). They remembered His holiness by the censer altar plates (Numbers 16:40). And they remembered their deliverance and specialness as a nation on the Sabbath (Deuteronomy 5:15). They were not only to give thanks to God for *what* He did but to give thanks for *how* He did it (Deuteronomy 8:1–18).

We can call this the Pattern of the Prodigal Son. Come back thankfully. Come back conscious of God's mercy. To keep this in our lives all the time is an inoculation against the doubt of forgetting how bad it is to be lost. In 1 Chronicles 16:35, one translation says, "To make thy praise our pride." The thing we're to be really proud about is that God is so wonderful.

Doubt comes when we take our eyes off God. He will withdraw the sense of His presence and everything will fall apart.

A Faulty Picture of God

Doubt number two is *a faulty picture of God.* Now it is areas like this in which material like John Dawson's awesome little tract for Last Days Ministries, "The Father Heart of God," has been greatly used. So many people have poor pictures of God. Some come from the fact that they just don't know what He is like and need to learn. Some come from the fact that they have been hurt perhaps as children by an ugly and unworthy picture of God. We all need to learn more about what God is really like. Too often, as J. I. Packer points out, we'll hear people say, "I like to think of God as . . .," which is usually followed by some idiocy. Who cares what you or I "like to think" about God? God is who He is. We are not to try to fit Him into our warped or inadequate notions, but to let the revelation of who He really is keep on correcting our vision. The greatest need of the twentieth-century Church is a fresh discovery of the greatness, glory, and goodness of God.

Weak Foundations

The third kind of doubt comes from *weak foundations*, from a poor understanding of truth. You got saved, which at the time seemed the obvious thing to do. You understood that God was real and you were lost. You then had a real experience with Christ. You just trusted Him; it was wonderful. If anyone asked you, you could testify to meeting Jesus. You knew *that* you believed, even a bit of *what* you believed, but above all you knew in *whom* you believed.

At this early level of Christian experience "Christian apologetics" probably means to you telling people you are sorry you did bad things to them! You might not know the issues. You might not know there even *are* any issues. Your primary concern is that the Gospel works, and perhaps later with how it works; you may never have had to even think about *why*.

If Christianity is true, it is supposed to have real answers to the problems of life. When we are first looking for answers from anything, we usually carry in mind two simple tests: (1) Does it seem to work? (pragmatic, practical) and (2) Does it make sense from where it starts to where it ends? (logical consistency within its premises, coherency).

Now if Christianity is true, we should see (perhaps in some-one else's life before our own) that it "works." We first find Christ a real answer for our felt and known needs. What we tried before did not last or did not satisfy. Our search for truth was on the basis of failed personal alternatives, not realized absolutes. Most of us meet Jesus on this first, pragmatic basis. We say, "I was into other things like ___ and ___ but my life was falling apart. Then I met Jesus and everything came together." Or, in the words of the old song, "I tried the broken cisterns, Lord, but, ah, the waters failed."

The truth is that Jesus is not only an "answer" to our needs. He is much more than even the real, sufficient, and only answer to *all* needs. First, Christ can meet our needs, but that is not why He is God. Jesus is much more than *an* answer, even more than *the* answer; He is the Lord of the universe, and we are to come to Him not just in needs, but in everything.

The second test, the "does it make sense?" question, usually isn't thought about until later. In this we come to the question of knowing who He is, and we can be freed from false pictures of Him by a growing, corrected revelation of His character that is both adequate and accurate. Here, when we have problems believing, we are dealing with doubt that comes from either being badly *taught* or badly *treated*. We can limit our vision of God and make Him too small, or we can live with a hurt that has damaged our idea of God and gives us a bad picture of Him. If our understanding of God's character is inadequate or inaccurate, incorrect or incomplete, we will experience doubt at this level.

But the facts that something "works" and "makes sense" within its premises are not the only tests for truth. There are after all a lot of things that seem both to "work" and to "make sense."

A devoted Buddhist lifestyle is a logical match for its philosophical tenets; a dedicated Muslim may live out the teachings of the Koran; even the hedonism and unabashed power-seeking of Satanism makes ugly, logical sense within its demonic premises. Hitler, too, accomplished things. Charles Manson made sense to his followers. Some things, like lies, are real but are not true.

So now we have to ask another question: *Is Christianity also true?* Does it make sense from where it starts to where it ends? Does it help? And now is it really true? We are going to be tested on that. We're telling other people in a world filled with competing ideas, principalities, and false gods that there is only "one Way" to heaven and only "one name under heaven" by which we may be saved. We are going to say to that world, "This is really true," so we are going to have to know something of the why. The bottom line is not that it "works," nor even that we can see how it "makes sense," but that it is true.

No matter how much we study or learn, of course, our knowledge of the "whys" and the "whats" of Christianity will never be exhaustive. We will never fully be able to know *all* the reasons; no finite being ever can or will. It does not mean that what we *do* learn is untrue; it just means there will always be more to learn, and there will be much more to the reason for what God says than we will ever know. Francis Schaeffer said we are like kids who've got our baby hands 'round the strings of a bunch of balloons. The balloons go all the way up. We don't have hold of the balloons; we have only the strings. We have no idea how many balloons are up there or what they all look like, but we really do have our fat little hands on the connections. What we have is true, even testably true, but not exhaustive. As eight-year old Anna of "Mr. God, This Is Anna," once said, "When you begin with the Answer, you can get a squillion questions right."

Why do we always have to put up with a partial revelation in which we always have to trust? Why doesn't God just come down and give us "no choice" but to believe? Why doesn't God just give us (as He no doubt could) overwhelming proof? Because that is not the rule of the game. "Overwhelming" is not the way God interacts with His children. Here's the God of the universe who knocks on your door. It is not: "Behold, I freak your head out and kick your door in." It is: "I stand at the door and knock" (Revelation 3:20).

It is in this area that we appreciate mystery because what we have is God who is utterly wonderful, yet reveals Himself in testable ways. I recently released a book on God that I've been working on for more than eighteen years. But it was not finished; it was *abandoned*. It never will be "finished." You never "finish" a book on God. In this world or the next, you will never stop thinking and learning about God.

So what if our basis for trust in God is not properly understood or solidly based? The best way to correct this kind of weak foundation is to do some reading and study. We must *do it*, not leave it for some expert or religious professional. Where are your own areas of inadequate or inaccurate vision? Find out for yourself. It will feed your faith to dig into some of the wonderful truths that await you. You will get excited to see just how powerfully the answers and evidences of the Gospel really are. There are many good books out today that deal with the facts and truth of the Christian faith. They deal with what we call "apologetics" or evidences for the truth of Christianity.

Josh McDowell has some excellent compilations in his writings on the truth of Scripture and the uniqueness of Christ in his best-selling books like *Evidence that Demands a Verdict*, *More Evidence that Demands a Verdict*, and *More than a Carpenter*. Michael Green and John Stott of England, John Warwick Montgomery, Clark Pinnock, Bernard Ramm, and Norman Geisler are just some of the scholars and theologians who have written powerful studies in apologetics that will be of help to you. Some of my favorites in this area are in the "Inklings," a small group of British literary figures who were also committed to Christ, like Dorothy Sayers, G. K. Chesterton, and C. S. Lewis. Thinkers from European ministries such as L'Abri like Os Guinness and the late Dr. Francis Schaeffer, men who minister in Eastern as well as Western cultures like Ravi Zacharias and the late E. Stanley Jones, have helped hundreds of thousands simply to reconsider the claims of Christ in the modern world.

Reading is an eternal investment, and study in this area will be deeply rewarding to you. If you are a parent, some of the most important and profound questions ever are not first mentioned in universities, but posed instead by your children. The best way to build truth into their lives is when they first ask, and you will find that you do not really understand something yourself until you are able to explain it to a child. On the job, important questions in life are always linked with the ultimate ones, and knowing some of the whys of Christianity will not only help you stay strong in your witness, but help you "give a reason for the answer that is in you." If you are an artist, a poet, or a musician, this will help develop your vision; you have a responsibility not just to be creative and moody, but to think deeply, too!

Sometimes people use Abraham and Isaac as an illustration of faith not involving any thinking, but that isn't true. It is precisely *because* Abraham knew *who* God was that he could trust Him in the dark when he didn't understand the *why*. He didn't know why, but he knew why he trusted God who did know why.

Faith without truth can pass as fantasy. How do you know that what you have is not fantasy? Perhaps this thing called Christianity is only a wish-fulfillment. What if you're just part of some sociological trend, some religious reaction to the emptiness, barenness, meaninglessness of our time? Truth is the answer to that. Faith without truth seems like fantasy. That is why a lot of kids are so cynical. They have no basis for trusting anyone or anything. In a *Roger Rabbit* world, when people are no longer able to distinguish between fantasy and reality, your best corrective after putting on display some working models of love and wisdom is a solid dose of truth.

Our Failure to Really Commit Ourselves

A lot of doubt begins here at this fourth most common cause of doubt. Commitment cements belief into conviction.

You only really believe something when you commit yourself to it. Have you ever met ex-church people who have dropped out? They will sometimes blame their defection on what they did or didn't believe, but that usually isn't the problem. The problem is, they don't want to commit themselves to what they found out was the truth.

I once talked to a young Red Guard who was actively promoting radical Communism in the West at a time when the Cultural Revolution in China was in its heyday and Chairman Mao was really hot news in the world. This guy had the armband, the button, the whole thing. He apparently once had some sort of church background, but had thrown it all away and embraced instead *The Little Red Book* and *The Thoughts of Mao*. For some reason he came to a service in which I spoke about commitment and happened to mention in passing the Red Guards. He came up to see me afterward to say what it meant to him to be a Mao follower. He said, "I don't believe in Jesus Christ. I don't believe in the Bible."

I said, "Have you read the Bible?"

He said, "Yes."

I said, "If you knew the Bible was true and that Jesus Christ really was God, would you have to make some major changes in the way you're living?"

He said, "Well, yes, I would."

I said, "It's not a question of whether you believe in Jesus and the Bible or not; it's a question of whether you really want to commit yourself to what you know. That's right, isn't it?"

He got very quiet. His eyes filled with tears and he said, "You don't understand. I train young people for Maoism in this country."

I said, "I really want to change the world, too. If Jesus were not who He said He was, and the Bible were not what it claimed to be, if there were no God and I was sure, I would probably be a Marxist or a Maoist like you. But the simple fact is that I cannot ignore the truth. I must deal with Christ. You know why it is easier to be a Marxist than to follow Jesus?

Because you can keep your selfishness and be a Maoist, but Jesus calls you to die."

Marxist thought requires unselfishness for revolution but cannot deliver it.

Failure to commit ourselves. We are to take truth and personal convictions seriously. How do you know if you really have convictions? You have to have an invisible sign hanging around your neck. (Mine reads, for instance: "This ministry is not for sale.") No conviction is truly your own unless you're prepared to hold it even if all others are against it.

I've sometimes told young Christians, "You need to follow Jesus even if everyone you know who is supposed to be a Christian turns his back on both Him and you." Here is a test of whether or not you really do hold a conviction. Can you say it succinctly, put it into a sentence? If not, it's just some vague idea. Can you put into a single statement, "This is what I am prepared to covenant with God"?

In Joshua 24:15 Israel's young leader calls the people to conviction: "Choose for yourselves this day whom you will serve." This was a situation of doubt for Israel, in which the people were called to make a decision. "Why," says Joshua, "do you stagger about between two things?"

Today we are called to make up our minds, and "put our money where our mouths are."

Daniel 3:16–18 gives us another wonderful insight into Christian doubt. Three boys are about to be thrown into a blast furnace. The king has had a sell-out concert. Everybody who was anybody in the whole Babylonian world was there, all the big bands were combined for this concert, and there was not an empty seat in the house. Everyone had to stand until the band played. Then everyone was supposed to bow. And they all did—all except three Hebrew guys who despite their extensive royal training did not seem to understand plain Babylonian.

They stood there alone and upright in the crowd and the king called them out. He said: "Don't you understand? If you don't bow, I'll throw you into this furnace!" (It's an extremely hot blast furnace, probably fired with bitumen and oxygen.) Nebuchadnezzar goes on. "You may be my favorite helpers, but this is embarrassing. You had better bow or you are going to burn. I am the king of the world and unless you show that you worship my statue along with everyone else I really will permanently take care of you."

What would you do? Would you smile and, so as not to offend, go ahead? Would you bow (certainly not enthusiastically) and mutter to yourself: "Well, God knows I am not really bowing 'in my heart.' After all, He has gone to all this trouble to put me in a place of some leadership and influence with these ungodly pagans and He certainly wouldn't want all that to come to an end now because of some silly little external show. I'll bow (outwardly only, of course) just to please the king, but God knows that it is all only an outward appearance. In my heart of hearts, am I not still following God?"

These boys didn't have the benefits of our modern understanding and could not adequately conceptualize some sort of contextual, cross-cultural, relational, and situational posture of influence. They had apparently also not yet learned how to spell *compromise* in either Hebrew or Babylonian. And this is what they said:

"If it be so our God whom we serve *is* able to deliver us. . . . But *if not.* . . ."

That *if not* is a Christian affirmation. It's doubt. It says, "I don't know if He will or not. I know He *can.* I *don't* know if He *will.*"

These boys knew who God was. They knew something of His wisdom, His character, and His power. They knew what He could do. They also knew some way or other, in life or by death, they would shortly be out of the king's power. They knew God could intervene. But they did not know, for them, for then, if God *would.* And knowing the king as they did, knowing that he would do exactly as he said, knowing fully the consequences of a polite but firm refusal, *they refused any-*

way: "But if not, we will not bow down." That's conviction. It has to do with commitment—even if you don't understand the whole thing, even if you don't know what's going on, even if you don't know what is going to happen to you. As Os Guinness says, weak convictions act on the drive train of faith like a slipping clutch.

Lack of Growth

Number five on the list of what brings on doubt is *lack of growth.* We have seen now the early reasons for experiencing doubt—having faulty *premises* as a Christian. The next two types of doubt have to do with our daily *practice* as Christians. This is not a problem of holding onto wrong ideas; it has to do with loss of freshness. One of the major reasons God will allow doubt in our lives is because we have not grown. Thirty years at one devotional level is not going to be sufficient if we hope to take on demons in a nation.

We're not talking about a deficiency in understanding about becoming a Christian but a deficiency in actual practice. Basically, it is this: We must always be developing a Christian world view. Ordinary living is a reality test for faith. This is why young people sometimes get wiped out spiritually even in a Bible college. They are not in the normal situations of life; they are often isolated from ordinary living. They don't meet real secular people who would challenge their small, smug answers and send them weeping back to God for something more. They don't run into people who have absolutely no concept about God and could not care less. If we want to win the world, we have to live in it and know both why and how it is lost. We need to rub shoulders often with people who, like ourselves once, are outside of God.

Some people are innocent in their rottenness. They have no great battles with spiritual claims. To them *"Jesus"* is only a swear word. They plow on in life apparently blind to spiritual reality until it hits them in the face. And often they are the easiest to win. Jesus really loved lost people who knew it, the drunks, the hookers, the rejected street people of His time. What He *said* and what He *was* struck them like spiritual lightning. It was said of Christ that He taught "as one having authority, and not as the scribes." He *lived.* He was full of goodness and compassion and excitement. Jesus did not seem to be religious; He was real.

Recently I was having lunch with a friend in a small Washington, D.C., hotel coffee shop. Out of the corner of my eye I noticed a man near us at a single table who seemed to be listening to our conversation, which revolved around some of the fun things God was up to in our lives. I didn't look at him, but from that point on I cut out of my vocabulary any specifically religious buzz words and kept on talking. The man finally finished his lunch, paid the bill, and left. But just minutes later he returned to his table and ordered a glass of water! He sat there sipping, ostensibly studying the door of the coffee shop, but gradually he moved his chair more and more around, until he was all but sitting facing us. Finally he could stand it no longer, and just plain interrupted. "Excuse me," he said, "I'm sorry to interrupt, but, hell, this is the most exciting thing I've ever heard!"

It turns out he was a businessman, a totally secular engineer with no spiritual background at all. He had known nothing about God and cared nothing about Him until his wife (who had apparently become a Christian) was killed in a car accident leaving him with two boys to bring up alone. It suddenly hit him that he had been relying on his wife to give the boys something spiritual; now that she was gone it was up to him. This man had never (as far as I was able to find out) been to a church; he wasn't going to one now. He knew less about God than the average seven-year-old Sunday school kid, but he had just gotten hold of a Bible and was reading it day and night. He was excited out of his mind with what he found. And this was the first time he had ever heard anyone else talking about it. God is constantly at work in His world.

What keeps you fresh? For me, it is keeping myself exposed to reality. Life is a reality test case. I've been out there 25 years saying, "Jesus is the answer." When I first said that, I didn't even know what the questions were. It's one thing to *say* something like that when you start, but it is quite another thing 25 years later still to be able to say the same thing, with ever-deepening conviction: "Jesus Christ really *is* the answer."

That answer must be practical, fresh, and contemporary. We either grow or we retreat. One reason doubt can creep in is that we're lazy. We don't want to grow. We're stuck where we are and contented. We're not constantly exposing ourselves to new risks, new ideas, new challenges. If you don't practice truth, after a while you begin to think that perhaps it is impractical. And truth that is impractical will soon be discarded as being untruth, and that's where doubt comes in.

Runaway Emotions

This sixth pathway to doubt is one most of us have faced but not understood. Doubt can come from *runaway or depleted emotions*. And I'm not just talking about Christians. There are Buddhists with runaway emotions who have doubts. There are atheists with used-up emotions who have severe doubts about atheism. It's a human problem, not a peculiarly Christian one. Everyone has doubts at times that stem from runaway emotions.

Doubt can sometimes be a good thing, because we live in a world that is fallen. This means that not everything is true though it often purports to be. Doubt doesn't buy at face value. So doubt doesn't have to be all bad; it can sometimes be good. The idea of *skeptic* comes from a word that means "to check it out," to investigate to find out if it's true or not.

But some doubt comes from emotional reaction and is not a mental or philosophical difficulty at all.

Let's look at a classic biblical example. We see Elijah (in 1 Kings 19:4) as a suicidal ninth century B.C. prophet. Imagine this: You have the most awesome experience of your entire life. A giant confrontation between God and Baal. All the priests of Baal come out. They're all there in force and there's just you (and Jehovah). There's the altar they built. They're dancing and cutting themselves with knives and crying out to Baal to answer by fire. Nothing is happening. People are getting a bit bored, so you provide a little side entertainment with suggestions like: "Better yell louder! Maybe your god went on a vacation. Perhaps he's on the toilet somewhere."

That's what Elijah yells to them all day . . . but they have no fire, nothing. They're ticked off. They've slashed their nice Sunday clothes to ribbons and nothing has happened. Then it is Elijah's turn. He rebuilds the altar of the Lord, digs a trench, and soaks the sacrifice in barrels and barrels of water. (There is always the skeptic in the audience who nods and says, "Ah. It was a rather hot day and rather dry wood. Spontaneous combustion. I've heard about it.")

Then Elijah prays a small prayer: "Lord, let it be known, I've done this according to Your word. Hear me that these people may know You are God." The fire falls, on the rocks, the bull, the water—everything. The fire licks up the bull, the rocks, the water in the trench, leaving just a big smoking hole, a lot of shocked Baal-worshipers, and a lot of very impressed Israelites. The people who are quite swift at recognizing the supernatural in this sort of thing all say: "The Lord, He is God!" (1 Kings 18:20–40).

After this supernatural act—the most awesome experience in Elijah's whole ministry—what do you think he is like from now on? A giant of faith? Far from it. This woman Jezebel puts a contract on his life and Elijah splits. When we find him, he's under a tree praying to die.

Isn't that the way it often is? *How is it that after the greatest experience of your whole life you suffer the greatest doubts and the greatest temptations?* Why is that?

The answer is simple. When you carry a huge amount of emotional intensity and then suddenly it drops, something snaps. It can be successes or failures. It can be after the greatest miracle of your life, or it can be when you're exhausted or lonely or tired or undernourished. Perhaps it's when you've suffered from a long illness, and an accident happens to you or a bereavement. Maybe you ve gotten really angry over something, or something doesn't turn out as you really wanted it to, or perhaps the problem is a battle with deep feelings of jealousy. All those things use emotions.

And when those emotions ebb, as they must, you can't handle it. There is this sense of numbness, of coldness, of loss. You feel empty, but cannot really see why. There is apparently no logical reason why you feel the way you do, but what you may lack in facts in this area at this time you can make up for in drama and imagination. There are no apparent reasons why you should be like this, but in your own mind you come up with one: "God is dead. Or if He is not dead, He has probably abandoned me." Your world has fallen apart. You can behave totally irrationally at this point, but it all makes sense to you . . . somehow!

Have you ever been in that situation? Isn't it a weird thing? There's apparently no reason for it. Something just snaps. You'd think after such an awesome demonstration of the power and presence of God in his life that Elijah would say, "Nobody is going to put out a contract on me! Fire fall on you, Jez." But here he is, the man of God, the one full of faith and power, asking for a quick death at the hands of God.

What is under fire here is not the *truth*, but individual *faith*. The facts are not the issue, not *what* you believe or *why* you believe it, but *how* you believe. Your own perception of truth is being challenged. The facts of what God is and what He says are not at all determined by what you know of Him now. It's not God's faithfulness, but your own faith that is in the fire, and in this case it is because your emotions have simply unloaded on you.

What is God's prescription for this? A refresher course on systematic theology, Divinity 1? A list of all the Scriptures that promise divine protection from demon-possessed queens in authority? Perhaps some stirring up of the prophet, something to keep him firmly reminded of his task and holy calling? Something in the order of:

"Elijah? What in the fat are you doing out here? Don't tell me after all I've done for you that you're afraid of one 'devil woman.' Get off your tail, cut out this pity-party, and get your act together. You get back to work. And, oh, Elijah, remember the fire that fell on the mountain? I can do that again, on anyone. Anytime I want to, remember. . . ."

No. You know what God does? *He bakes a cake for him* (1 Kings 19:5–8).

You sit down and pray that He will kill you and He brings you a cake! He says, "Have a little rest, all right?" What kind of God is this?

The answer to this kind of doubt from shattered emotions is not to increase your religious activity, but just *rest and relax*. Take a break. Play. If you're doubting because you're tired, the answer is not to pray more, but to sleep. Overwork may not need a spiritual heart search but a day off at the beach— maybe three days off at the beach.

There are ministers who have driven themselves to burnout because they feel the responsibility of always being spiritual for other people and no longer have time to enjoy being saved themselves. There are housewives who suffer a crisis of faith. They cannot understand why they feel the way they do about God. The fact that their new baby is crying at odd hours of the night and their two-year-old is wrecking the house does not have anything much to do with it. It's just that their weekly requests for prayer at the ladies' luncheon (sent in by proxy because they are too tired to go) do not seem to be relieving the pressure. But the answer here is not intensified religious activity but relief of the pressure and relaxation.

It always amazes me how much material Charles Haddon Spurgeon put out. From the time he was seventeen he just churned out words. My Spurgeon library in New Zealand takes up an entire wall of thick volumes, with thousands of sermons in his *Metropolitan Tabernacle Pulpit* alone, not to mention his *Treasury of David, Lectures to My Students.* . . . He just preached and preached. Yet I hear that every summer he went down to the beach and snorkeled and lay around in the sun. Then he went back to his pulpit full of fire and fresh zeal and put out all this material that is still ministering to people a century after his death.

It is as much a command of God that we *rest* as that we do not commit adultery. Yet sincere and godly people who would not think of lying or stealing or dishonesty, let alone murder or immorality or blasphemy, habitually and regularly violate this divine provision. They are to be found grim-lipped and devout, continually pushing themselves beyond their human limits, meanwhile quoting to themselves and others various sacred imprecations like "I'm not going to rust out, I'm going to burn out . . . for God."

The "for God" is always added for its devotional overtones. Without it, the drive might be recognized for what it often is: ambition, guilt, or religious fantasy posing as spirituality. Burn out, not rust? Go ahead. The only difference between rust and fire is time. Both are the results of oxidation; one just goes quicker than the other. When the wick in a lamp starts to burn, the lamp is running out of oil. And the solution is not more fire, or a lament for the wick, but more oil. Sons and daughters of God are led, not driven.

Sometimes we lose it all because we are wound up and overburdened and this becomes a major crisis in our faith. We say, "I don't know what to do. Heaven is blank." Have a sleep! Eat a cake! And after a couple of treatments of this, God shares some things with Elijah that will help put him back on the track to finish his course.

The rest and food first. This is not the final or only answer, of course. We must learn as well to recognize this sort of doubt and learn to retrain our emotions so we don't get overwhelmed in situations like this. When this happens, we have a short-term answer: Take a break. But we can also work on a long-term answer: Learn not to trust your feelings and thoughts in such situations, as they often run wild. Understand that when it comes, as it came to Elijah, that emotional overload may be the reason for your doubt. Learn that you can have those times.

They Doubted For Joy

This last one is probably the hardest of all to handle. When the disciples saw Jesus return from the dead, Scripture (Luke 24:41, RSV) says: "They disbelieved [doubted] for joy." What does that mean? It means this: You want so much to believe in the unexpected good news that to discover it isn't true would just totally destroy you. It is a doubt that comes in the very area you most want to believe, because of some hurtful experience in the past.

They saw Him die! For a long time it was just talk. Jesus said: "I'm going to be taken. I'm going to be crucified." They said to themselves: "Oh, yes. He'll be crucified but at the last minute the nails will come out by miracle, the messianic reign will begin, and we'll, of course, be there to share in it."

And then He didn't do it. He didn't fight. He let Himself be laid down and the Romans did nail Him up and He really did die. The soldier put the spear into His side and the blood really came out and He really was dead. And the disciples wrapped His body themselves and they laid Him in the grave. Talk about doubt! They were devastated. I'm sure some of them thought about packing it all in and going back, some-how, if they could, to their old lives.

But suddenly there on the shore was someone who looked awfully much like Jesus and they couldn't believe it. They wanted so much to believe it was true, but they couldn't. They couldn't believe it because they knew it was the very thing they most *wanted* to believe. What if it turned out only as another crazy wish-fulfillment fantasy, like the one they just had followed? Jesus had said He was the Messiah. They had seen the miracles and the love and the power and they had believed He would rule the world. But then they had seen Him really die and all their dreams had come crash-ing down in the dust.

Now there was someone standing on the shore that unac-countably looked like Him and sounded like Him, but how could it be? Their fresh scars were in danger of being ripped again, this time for good.

That is probably the hardest one of all. In all of our lives there is usually one place that still hurts. There's one place still sealed. There's one place where final healing has not been allowed, one place that we keep away from complete openness. We would love to believe it. It is the one thing *we most want* to believe out of anything and everything we have ever wished. But what if with all our hopes at their highest, it doesn't turn out to be true after all? It would be the final devastation. It would hurt so much we would never recover. So we don't want to think about it. We don't want to talk about it. Leave us alone, okay? We don't want to look at that figure on the shore. We're not able to receive.

And what have we done? We have let a problem take God's place and become the controlling principle of our lives. So our problem becomes our idolatry. And in the best of polite, sad, well-chosen spiritual words I may say to myself: *Well, I'd really like to believe that. It's true, I suppose, for some peo-ple, but I can't look because (though I'd never tell another living soul) I'm afraid it won't be true.* So the problem becomes god to us. We look at God through the eyes of the problem instead of looking at the problem through the eyes of God. We won't let Him be God in the situation, and it becomes the secret, absolute center of our whole lives.

What is the answer to this last sort of doubt? First of all, get that doubt out in the light. Perhaps write it down on paper so you know exactly what it is. You've lived with it hidden too long. Articulate your doubt; make sure you know clearly what it is and what it isn't. "This is what I am most afraid of. I really wish this were true, but I don't know if it is." Identify it so that it's not some lion lurking in your subconscious ready to pounce on you.

When C. S. Lewis went through that terrible time of watching his wife, Joy Davidman, die, he went through real doubt. He said that during that time of doubt, it wasn't that he doubted that God wouldn't turn out to be there after all, but that maybe God would not turn out to be the God that Lewis had always thought he was. "Sooner or later," he said, "I must face the question in plain language. What reason have we except our own desperate wishes to believe that God is, by any standard we can conceive, 'good'? . . . I wrote that last night. It was a yell rather than a thought. Let me try it over again. Is it rational to believe in a bad God? Anyway, in a God as bad as all that?"

Lewis went on to say in *A Grief Observed* that too-human pictures of God forged during hurt and grief leave no room for "something older than yourself, something that knows more, something you can't fathom." In the preservation of mystery there is hope. If by some sort of "extreme Calvinism" our fears of God being unreasonable, vindictive, vain, unjust, and cruel were urged on us as "actually true but count as virtue in Him," we would lose all our basis of thinking and living. Then reality is in its very root meaningless, and "what is the point of trying to think about God or anything else? This knot comes undone when you try to pull it tight."

"The doubt of joy" is a hard one because we want so much

to believe that God is really the way that He says He is. But what if He really isn't? What if I trust in that area and am devastated again?

What does Jesus do? It's a beautiful thing. He's there on the beach doing the most ordinary thing. He is cooking breakfast! He does something so simple, so common, so natural. He doesn't glow with light from another world, float out toward them in the boat, and speak with a voice enhanced by heavenly echo chamber. He eats breakfast. *Ghosts don't eat fish.* What He does is give them a whole fresh context, and that's what you need for this final area. You've got to step out of the circle of your own pain for a moment and see things in a totally different light. In the disciples' minds, it can't possibly be Jesus. He's dead. This is a ghost, some alien.

Yet He stands there and says, "Have you had breakfast yet?" And He eats. And something shifts deep inside and they suddenly see. "He really is alive! He really is!"

7

Elijah at Kidron: When the Brook Dries Up

Elijah was a man taken care of by God when the land was under His judgment. Although drought and famine filled the nation of Israel, Elijah was fed supernaturally. Although Christians may share to some extent in the consequences of a judgment that comes on a nation because of sin, God's provision and care continue for the individuals, in this case the prophet.

Then the brook dried up.

Why did it happen? And what do you do when supernatural provision stops?

Henry Sloane Coffin looked at this theme in his 1930s message *Inspirations that Fail*. If we were to paraphrase and amplify that message in the light of the situations of our time, it might look something like this: God has a course for His children. Everyone's curriculum is different. The only thing that remains the same is its *aim:* to keep you confident in *depending on resources outside of yourself.*

Elijah was a man who knew how to hear from heaven. He was a man we recognize as the greatest of all the prophets of the Old Testament. He knew how to talk to God, and he knew how to listen. A bad king gave a series of bad calls, and Elijah's response under God was to face that king with the consequence of his sin and to tell him that God was going to bring judgment (1 Kings 16:30–32, 17:1).

Judgment on the Nation

Elijah's word to the king was that the heavens would give no rain and though, as James says, he was a man of "like passions as we are," he "prayed earnestly . . . and it rained not on the earth by the space of three years and six months" (James 5:17, KJV). If we do not listen to His Word, God has, of course, other ways of getting our attention. There are four major ways in which God can bring up judgment on a country (Ezekiel 14:13–23).

First, through the economy: He can "cut off the supply of bread." Money gets tight, food and water are in short supply, essentials get scarce. Sometimes people start thinking seriously about God only when things start going wrong.

Second, through ecology: He can "cause wild beasts to pass through the land." God is sovereign Ruler of the whole creation. Even one small creature let loose in the judgment of God can fell a ruler. For Pharaoh it was frogs, lice, flies, and locusts; for others it might be a wasp, an ant, a medfly. It could be a change in weather, in the relationship of the sun or (in Elijah's case) the dew and the rain. The worldwide concern over the greenhouse effect may not just be about fluorocarbons and exhaust emissions. When the very air and weather begin to change in unpredictable ways, people start thinking about their own personal behavior. For Egypt, the pests were a testimony to the fact that something was supernaturally wrong in their land. For Israel in Ahab's day, the drought was a sign of the displeasure of God.

Third, through disease: He can "send a pestilence." When God removes His hand of protection from a nation something too small to see begins to bring sentence on whole cities. There are yet more dangerous plagues possible than AIDS; sometimes people begin to take eternity seriously only in the face of incurable illness. In Naaman's leprosy he sought God; in Herod's death great fear came on the court.

Fourth, through civil or international war: He can "bring a sword on that land."

It has happened in history before and it can happen again. When we do not listen, the judgment of God can "bring a sword"—that is, He removes His peace from a country and allows another nation to invade or go to war with the land.

Elijah was a man who lived in a nation, like some of us today, under divine judgment. People were hurting financially. Jobs were lost, crime was on the rise, people were struggling. There was political division, collapse of leadership, bad public examples, murder, and suicides. The land was in famine; but through it all Elijah was personally taken care of. God faithfully provided food and water every day; He commanded the ravens to bring meat, and the river kept running (1 Kings 17:3–6).

No one has all he needs in himself. Elijah needed the brook and the birds. And no one can live a truly independent life. Besides basic physical needs like food and water and shelter we all have other needs. "Blessed are the poor in spirit," Jesus said, "for theirs is the kingdom of heaven." A genuinely *poor* person has no resources in himself to meet essential needs. And no one, especially not a man or woman of God, has all the required wisdom, abilities, and means. As John Donne wrote, "No man is an island."

We tend to focus on people or situations or things that seem to meet those needs: friends, teachers, books, ideas, a place, a work, a church. A *friend* can stimulate our minds, satisfy our hearts, and stir our souls. A *teacher* can catch our admiration, awaken our appreciation, push open a mental door for us to new realms. A *book* we come across might capture our imagination, reset our priorities, restructure our whole world view. A *place* we live in can become a home, a castle, a refuge, a security that sends us out armed with determination and courage and welcomes us back to rest and sympathy. Our *work* can be the dominant drive of our lives, giving us a reason to get up in the morning with purpose and vision. Our *church* might be the focus of our hopes and ideals, the friendship and encouragement of others much like us who are learning life together. Or we may be gripped by a *great idea* that lights up our whole world with a vision of what can be done. All these and more may be to us as a river of God full of water.

When the Brook Runs Dry

Imagine what it was like for Elijah. Each day his every need had been met. He never had to worry like the rest of the nation where his next meal was coming from. God was in charge of things, God was going to take care of him. All he had to do was trust and pray and wait. And then one day the brook dried up.

What happened to Elijah can happen to us. Things or people we relied on, depended on, built our lives around suddenly change, move on, or move away.

Your *friend* is still your friend; but somehow, insensibly, you have grown apart and now it seems irreversible. It is not that you have quarreled; it is just that now your paths are moving in different directions. You may see him or her almost as much as before, but somehow it now seems less. It is sad and it wrenches at something deep inside you, but there is really nothing either of you can do. Just like the brook, the water you once drew from in your friend's life has dried up.

You still get to hear your *teacher*, but the man at whose feet you sat in wonder at twenty you may have outgrown at thirty or forty. It is not that what he says is now no longer true; it is just that you judge things more critically now. You have grown. You see things somewhat differently with the passage of the years.

That *book* moved you once, and perhaps it still does; but

you do not care to read it over again and again. Many like it have passed from dominating your thoughts and attention into pleasant and sometimes quaint memories; like old songs they have moved into nostalgia and history.

Maybe you return to the *place* you loved and remembered before but to your surprise, everything is changed. Someone else lives there now and he has made it almost unrecognizable. Perhaps the house where you lived is gone, or it has become, by neglect or disaster, a ruin. Or circumstances have changed and you must move somewhere else, find another home, change everything you were always so contented with: The brook dries up.

The *work* you are still doing but is it the same for you now? Maybe you can keep on doing it until you die; some do. But then again, perhaps the brook here, too, has dried up. Perhaps your job is gone now. They did not need you any longer. Either someone else has filled the ranks instead or you can no longer do what you did before.

The *ministry* you were given: Is it coming to an end?

And your *church*, the place that was such a haven for your spirit: What has happened there? It is not as if it had to split or fail; it may still be as before, perfectly able to meet others' needs. It may be simply that *for you* it has somehow lost its appeal. The water from which you drew has been diverted to other side channels. The people you were close to have moved, the pastor has changed, the ministry you previously relied on has begun to dissolve or disband. It hurts, it is uncomfortable to think about, it bothers you deeply, but the outcome is certain: The brook has dried up.

But you, like Elijah, should know this could happen to anyone. It can happen over anything we try to count on always being close to us. It happened *even to Jesus*. There was a time when He couldn't rely on His friends, His family, His ministry, His home church, or even His best and closest disciples.

There were things happening to Him that weren't in the

Book He knew and loved from childhood. Of His ministry He said, "My meat is to do the will of Him that sent Me and to finish His work," but there were times when even He could do nothing.

He had grown up going to the synagogue. He had been the central focus of the teachers there when He was only twelve. Then later, giving His first personal message, what He said came into violent conflict with the elders and they "cast Him out."

There came a day even to Christ when His family seemed to fail Him, when He was misunderstood and interfered with, when even His relatives told people that He was out of His mind. There came a time when He said, "The foxes have holes and the birds of the air have nests, but the Son of Man has nowhere to lay His head."

And there came an awful hour when He could not rely on even His closest friends. The disciples went to sleep during His agony of prayer and the man He had called "friend" sold Him to His enemies for thirty pieces of silver.

There was even that one frightening moment when it seemed as if the Great Vision that moved Him all His life hung in the balance. In Gethsemane He prayed, "Father, if it be possible, let this cup pass from Me." And on the cross He cried, "My God, My God, why have You forsaken Me?"

If it happened to Elijah, if it happened to Jesus, it will no doubt happen also to you.

No One Should Possess a Private Brook

All the land is drought and famine but Cherith is still flowing when Israel is dry. What would have happened to Elijah if the stream had kept on flowing?

(1) His blessings would have become a barrier. Elijah "was a man of like passions" but it certainly doesn't seem like it. This man is like something out of a fantasy movie—some holy

Lawrence of Arabia figure, twice as large as life, not your average Christian! The brook *had* to dry up. God was behind it. That is what happens; people need to be reminded they are ordinary after all. The godly especially sometimes become inhuman. They find the invisible so satisfying they are hard on their fellow mortals.

What might have happened day after day sipping from the cold stream when all the land was parched and dying? Elijah might have lost his prophet's sympathy for people. He might have been tempted to take the attitude, "People are starving and thirsty, but they deserve it. If they would only learn, like me, to trust God they wouldn't be in such a mess."

(2) His privileges might have turned to pride. Elijah had a high standard for his own life. Like all prophets he knew what is expected of the godly. As a child he had great dreams. He had no doubt set his heart as a boy to be the very best he could be. To fail that calling in any way is for an Elijah utterly devastating. Later in his life Jezebel put out a contract on his life and Elijah the fearless prophet ran away. The sense of failure so overwhelmed him that he wanted to die.

His words reveal the danger of a high self-set standard that is somehow compromised: "It is enough! Now, Lord, take my life, for *I am no better than my fathers!*" (1 Kings 19:4). Did he really think he was? The brook *had* to dry up. Elijah had to be reminded that the only thing that makes us special is that we are made in God's image, and the only thing that sets us apart is the grace of God.

(3) His rest might have made him a permanent recluse. We all need time to recover from the pressures of life; it is part of both the design and commandment of God to take off from daily labor. Jesus told His disciples to "sit by the well and rest." "Come ye apart," the old adage says, "or ye will come apart." But too long in the safety and shelter and security of Cherith may have worked to hurt him instead of help him. Elijah may have become content to stay near Horeb supplied by God and quit the battle. God is out to do three things, said

an old writer: "Get us out of the world, get the world out of us, and then send us back into the world." No one can live forever at Cherith.

Elijah Driven to Zarephath

Here is a man who has challenged the might of kings, a solitary man who has stood alone unaided by anyone except God. All through his life and ministry he has been dependent on no one but God, and needed nothing but God's word. But now that word comes to him and calls him to a place of embarrassment: He is to go to a home for shelter and sustenance where a widow and her son are about to make their last meal before they starve to death.

Sometimes your Cherith must fail in order to force you to hurt with other people. If the brook had kept on flowing Elijah might have counted on it and forgotten the God who gave it. *The means by which God maintains us are always in danger of becoming the barriers that shut us out from Him.* Cheriths can't be permanent.

Now, more than ever, we live in a future shock world. Nothing seems to last. People change; friends come and go; the world keeps shifting gears. Best-selling books are now in bargain bins. Ideas change as fast as rock stars and we are wholly not the same people we were ten years ago. Thomas Hardy wrote: "It is the ongoing of the world that makes it sad. If the world stood still at a happy moment there would be no sadness in it. The sun and moon standing still on Ajalon was not a catastrophe for Israel but a type of paradise."

But a stationary heaven or earth would become dull at last. All change is risky, but some change must come. God has given us seasons. Without the winter, summer's warmth would not be as welcome; the reds and golds of fall set off the coming green freshness of spring. And so with the seasons of our spirit; each is necessary for all the colors and flowers of our lives.

Don't mourn your Cheriths. *In the growth of your spirit, the next is always better.* Thank God for what they meant to you as reminders of His love and move on. You will one day see the hand of God in the drying up of your brook. The dwindling of the stream will mean in time not only help for you, but help for others. Elijah left Cherith for Zarephath, not only to save a mother's life, but to learn something more of God's love. A brook and birds don't show you as much of God as a mother and a child. And though you may miss your brook, you will not miss God; your new course will take you all the way from the valley to a foretaste of Bethlehem.

Prayer

O Jesus, we thank You. We thank You for the river that rises, touching our loins, and we thank You for the river we are going to hit that we can't swim in anymore. It will carry us. We can't carry it. It is a river not only that we can't pass over, but that cannot be passed over. We thank You for calling us to abandonment to You, to being swept along, not in chaos, not in the same thing we were in long, long ago, but in a sense of abandonment to the purposes of the river. We believe out of this river will come healing wherever it goes.

So we pray that You will take our own doubts, our own struggles and suffering, and translate these into life. Feed this river, we pray, with our own suffering and our own struggle for the help of others who may face probably the scariest time in our century with courage and joy and faith.

Level Four

Waters to Swim In

"Blessed are they that have not seen and yet have believed."
—Jesus to Thomas

Again he measured a thousand; and it was a river that I could not ford, for the water had risen, enough water to swim in, a river that could not be forded.   Ezekiel 47:5, NAS

8

Abandonment to Mystery

And now the last stage of the river—the scariest stage of all. All the while the river is rising, first flowing under the door, to the *ankles*, to the *knees*, to the *loins*. And now, at last, to the very limit; it is no longer something you can carry, it is something that must carry you. The last step in God is one that takes you beyond your own control.

Our Call to Abandonment

We all should know what it means to surrender to Christ, but *how deep does that surrender go?* Ezekiel faced something that was finally beyond his limit. The previous measures into the river were all right; they could be managed, handled, accommodated. But now this was the end of wading. He knew he could not ford this crossing; it was now bigger than he was.

Do we really know our limits? A characteristic of our Western culture is our deep need to be able to control our own lives, to be able to get a handle on everything we meet. In the U.S. Bill of Rights every citizen under the government of this nation is guaranteed protected personal rights; but in the Bible mandate, every citizen of heaven under the government of God is called to give up the self-protection of his or her rights and come wholly under the provision, care, and shelter of Another. We are not used to being unable to control things; it bothers us intensely when things happen that we cannot manage. But to meet and follow the living God is to deliberately hand over the reins of your life to Another. As the bumper sticker says, "If God *is* your co-pilot—switch seats."

Ezekiel's call to the last level was not, however, a situation of despair. It was too high for walking, but it was high enough now to swim in. God always calls us, as Catherine Marshall said, "beyond our selves." Nothing of faith is ever quite safe.

We have a habit of looking at things out of our depth as barriers instead of possibilities, as signposts of discouragement instead of opportunities to trust and learn. We firmly resist things we have never attempted: "No, thanks; I can't do that." But there is so much that God wants us to do that we cannot do ourselves. When we run out of our natural resources, God is ready to show us His supernatural ones. And risk, challenge, adventure are the heart of all growth and life. It is in the early shallows of the river that our first tests come; if we are not found faithful there, what will happen to us when the river really rises? Whether we like it or not, situations and circumstances will come to us like Ezekiel's river, in which we will either have to learn to swim or drown.

> "If you have run with the footmen, and they have wearied you, then how can you contend with horses? And if in the land of peace, in which you trusted, they wearied you, then how will you do in the flooding of the Jordan?"   Jeremiah 12:5

A. J. Gossip was a famous preacher at the turn of the century. Like his congregation, he too had his share of shock and the unexpected floods of life; yet in the midst of his own great personal grief and hurt, he was still expected to minister and be a comfort and blessing to others. In 1927 after his beloved wife died, Gossip preached a message from this text in Jeremiah that he called "But When Life Tumbles In, What Then?"

It is one thing, Gossip said, to complain to God about the bewilderment of life when all you have faced are the "little rubs and frets and ills of life that fall to everyone."

[But] if these have broken through your guard, pushed aside your religion, made you so sour and peevish and cross toward God—God help you. What will happen when sudden as a shell screaming out of the night, some one of the great crashing dispensations bursts in your life and leaves an emptiness where there had been a home, a tumbled ruin of your ordered ways, a heart so sore you wonder how it holds together? If you have caught your breath, poor fool, when splashing through the shallow waters of some summer brook, how will you fare when Jordan bursts its banks and rushes as far as the eye can see, one huge wild swirl of angry waters and you, your feet caught away, half-choked, you are tossed nearer and nearer to the roaring of the falls and over it? . . .

Do you think Christ always understood or found it easy? There was a day when He took God's will for Him in His hand and turned it round and looked at it. And, "Is this what You ask of Me?" He said and for a moment His eyes looked almost incredulous. And another day, puzzled and uncertain, He cried out, "But is this really what You meant that I should give You, this here, this now?" Yes and another still, when the cold rushing waters roared in a raging torrent through His soul; yet He would not turn back, fought His way to the further bank, died still believing in the God who seemed to have deserted Him. And that is why He is given a name that is above every name. . . . You people in the sunshine *may* believe the faith, but we in the shadow *must* believe it. We have nothing else. . . .

[And when] standing in the roaring of Jordan, cold to the heart with its dreadful chill, and very conscious of the terror of its rushing, I too, like Hopeful, can call back to you who one day in your turn will have to cross it: *"Be of good cheer, my brother, for I feel the bottom and it is sound."*

9

A River that Could Not Be Passed Over

Notice how much this last level in our scriptural lives looks like the first; we are not in control of ourselves. At the level of chaos we are at the mercy of our own lusts; at the level of mystery we are at the mercy of the Lord Himself. At the first stage of chaos we are borne along by something we cannot control; like Paul we can say, "What I will to do, that I do not practice; but what I hate, that I do" (Romans 7:15). Our lusts are lord of our lives. The river rises all the time, from chaos to principle to doubt and now to mystery; and now at this last stage, too, we are no longer in charge. We are about to be carried along by someone who has a far higher and better purpose than just letting us do what we want.

And as Ezekiel noticed, it *"could not be crossed."* It was not just something beyond his own personal limits—"I could not pass over"; it was something beyond anyone's personal limits. What God has in mind is not for some special saint, some rare individual with unique gifts and calling. God is out to bring His people all to the end of their limits; this is a river no one can pass over.

This stage takes you beyond your own control of things. It not only answers the questions, it takes you beyond the questions because it is touching something more than you can

133

comprehend. It is called *abandonment*. It is the level of loving service that all the great saints and lovers of God sought and many experienced over the centuries that made them strong in the face of great hardship and difficulty.

A Thirst for God

A book was published centuries ago called *The Cloud of Unknowing*. It was written in the Europe of the fourteenth century, a time of great distress, social unrest, and violent insurrection. There was famine, war, and terrible plagues. In England the Black Death killed multitudes, including many of the clergy and ministers of that time, spiritually impoverishing the world.

Yet this terrible century produced at the same time some of the greatest contemplative Christian saints and mystics of the Church, who not only "possessed their souls in peace," but wrote of their experiences with God with profound thought, vivid expression, and contagious enthusiasm.

Richard Rolle, Lady Julian of Norwich, John Tauler, Henry Suso, and St. Catherine of Siena were some of the greatest devotional writers of the Church. They all lived joyously, even radiantly through this same time. They were not just a few odd hermits and recluses; they were practical men and women with active lives and sometimes major responsibilities in leadership and society.

Not all the depths they explored are recommended or even advised for everyone; they took pains to point out that God calls people into a work, that the effort itself depends on God, that it is "never gotten by study, but only by grace," and that it is a mistake to imagine all Christians are to apply themselves in the same way. Indeed, most of them were at a loss to explain or recommend methods, principles, and approaches o others, as it was their conviction that God alone would provide for each individual.

"He is a jealous lover," wrote the author of *The Cloud*, "and suffereth no fellowship; He liketh not to work in thy will unless He be only with thee by Himself. He asketh no help but only thyself. He wills thou but look on Him and let Him alone." They knew only that the key to entering into the mystery of God Himself was to set the heart on loving God past our human limits of understanding Him, that this devotion should not be "artificial or violent, but spring gently and sweetly from love to love."

They all shared this one thing in common: a thirst for God and a depth of desire for Him that is largely missing in our shallow century. Their writings show us that "in spite of all this, and perhaps because of all this—a man could possess his soul in peace and that there were many more like him. They are evidence that through all difficulties there persisted a Christian life which was superior to secular disturbance . . ." (from the introduction of *The Cloud of Unknowing*).

Into the Depths of Mystery

Mystery. The Bible is full of it. The *Kingdom of God* operates in "mystery" (Mark 4:11). *Lawlessness* is called a "mystery" (2 Thessalonians 2:7) and so is *godliness* (1 Timothy 3:16). The *Church* is a mystery (Ephesians 5:32). The *Gospel* operates in mystery (Ephesians 6:19; 1 Corinthians 1:17–25). The *resurrection* is a mystery (1 Corinthians 15:51) and *God Himself*, our Uncreated Triune Creator, is the ultimately Mysterious One (Colossians 2:2).

But *mystery* in the Bible does not mean quite the same thing as it means to most people today. *Mystery* in the dictionary primarily signifies something hidden, withheld, strange, or secret; Oxford defines it as a "hidden or inexplicable matter." Mystery, of course, does mean this, but it means something more in the Bible; it is spiritual truth divinely revealed. Although mystery is something only God can show us, it is something He *can* show us. Mystery is indeed a secret; but in the revelation of God, it is an "open" secret.

Mystery, says Vine's *Expository Dictionary*, simply denotes "something outside the range of natural unassisted apprehension." Mystery is something you can't grasp with just personal study, effort, and training; mystery is something you cannot know at all unless God shows you "in a manner and at a time appointed by God and to those only who are illumined by His Spirit. . . . In the ordinary sense, mystery implies knowledge withheld; its Scriptural significance is truth revealed" (*Expository Dictionary of New Testament Words*).

In mystery, the divine plan is concealed from all until God's time and even then revealed only to His chosen; but He does show His purpose to the right people at the right time. And what is the foundation, the secret, the heart of receiving any such divine revelation? Not knowledge, but *love*.

"He who has My commandments and keeps them," said Jesus, "it is he who loves Me. And he who loves Me will be loved by My Father, and I will love him and manifest Myself to him" (John 14:21). Notice: *A manifestation of Christ to the soul follows the obedience of love.* Not knowledge first, but love. Not information as a start, but devotion. Not understanding to begin with, but abandonment. Indeed, without that love, even an exceptional degree of religious insight is worthless. "Though I speak with the tongues of men and of angels," said Paul, ". . . and though I have the gift of prophecy, and understand all mysteries and all knowledge . . . but have not love, I am nothing" (1 Corinthians 13:1–2).

God, who is the Maker of both the power to love and to know, says the unknown author of *The Cloud of Unknowing*, is to the knowing power alone "ever more incomprehensible": but to the loving power "He is, in every man diversely, all comprehensively to the full. . . . One loving soul, alone in itself, by virtue of love, may comprehend in itself Him who is sufficient to the full—and much more without comparison—to fill all the souls and angels that ever may be.

And this is the endless, marvelous miracle of love, the working of it which shall never have end; forever shall He do it and never shall He cease for to do it. See who so by grace may see; for the feeling of this is endless bliss and the contrary is endless pain."

It is, he says, *the work of the soul that most pleases God.* All the saints and angels "have joy of this work and hasten them to help it with all their might; all friends be mad when you do thus, and try to defeat it in all that they can. . . . Have no wonder that I stir thee to this work. For this is the work . . . in which man should have continued if he had never sinned. And to this working was man made, and all things for man to help him and further him to it. And by this working shall man be repaired again. And for want of this working a man falls ever more deeper and deeper into sin and further and further from God."

Learning How to Swim

I learned to swim in a New Zealand primary school. At least, I was *supposed* to learn. What actually happened is that I splashed impressively with my arms, kicked with one foot, and hopped along the bottom with the other; it looked like swimming and it passed for it as long as we were in our shallow little school paddling baths. Fine, as long as there was a bottom I could always feel and touch.

Then one day my aunt took my younger sister and me to a country swimming hole. A narrow ledge of rock went out from the bank for a few feet before a big drop-off into the dozen-foot-or-so-deep hole. I was hopping along this narrow ledge kicking and saw a long branch lying near me in the water. I thought, *I can probably hold onto that stick and float with it.* So I grabbed the stick and continued kicking along the ledge until I suddenly ran out of rock. My foot went off the end, I lost the branch, and went under. The next second I was drowning.

I didn't know how to swim. I had had the illusion of swimming as long as I had one foot on the bottom, but now it was the real thing. There was nothing left to stand on. They say your life passes before you die; I was only little, so mine passed very fast. The next thing I remember was being pulled out of the water by one of my aunt's boyfriends, who had just happened to notice me going under for the last time.

And you—have you had the floor pulled out from under you? In this area of mystery, God takes the ledge away from us in order to bring us into reality. Like children, we have hopped too long with one foot on the bottom, secure in the illusion that we were really swimming; now there is no bottom to touch in this river, and we find out just how much of our splashing around was only a show. The river is rising, and we are not to be children forever.

"Right well have you said," noted the author of *The Cloud*, " 'for the love of Jesus.' For in the love of Jesus shall be your help. Love is such a power that it makes all things to be shared. Therefore we love Jesus, and all things that He has are thine."

This love, of course, is not a feeling; it is an act of will. *Agape* love in the Bible is an unselfish choice for the highest good; of God first, and then His creation. You can love with this love when you do not like; you can choose when you cannot feel; and you can set your heart on pleasing God when you cannot comprehend.

"For of all other creatures and their works—yea, and the work of God Himself—may a man through grace have fullness of knowing, and well can he think of them; but of God Himself can no man think," reports *The Cloud*. "And therefore I would leave all that thing that I can think, and choose to my love that thing I cannot think. For why, He may well be loved, but not thought. By love He may be gotten and holden; but by thought neither. . . .

"And although it be a light and a part of contemplation, nevertheless in this work it shall be cast down and covered with a cloud forgetting. And thou shalt step above it stalwartly, but listily [with pleasure or delight], with a devout and a pleasing stirring of love, and try to pierce that darkness above thee. And smite upon that thick cloud of unknowing with a sharp dart of longing love; and go not hence for aught that befalleth."

10

All-Out Faith

What does it mean to trust Christ? Blondin (Jean-François Gravlet) was a famous acrobat and tightrope-walker in the nineteenth century. His most famous achievement was crossing Niagara Falls by tightrope, usually without a safety net. He did it many times in different ways: blindfolded, in a sack, on stilts, even sitting down to make and eat an omelette and make a cup of coffee with a primus stove and water drawn up from the river!

Perhaps one of his most daring feats was to push a wheelbarrow loaded with a heavy sack of cement across the wire. With all that weight, the slightest overbalance could wrench the barrow out of his hand or twist him off the wire and into the river. But Blondin, the supreme showman of that time, was the master of the high wire; he took the wheelbarrow all the way across without a hitch.

After one such successful stunt, Blondin asked an impressed reporter: "Do you believe I can do anything on a tightrope?" "Oh, yes, Mr. Blondin," said the reporter, "after what I've seen today I believe it. You can do anything."

"Do you believe, then," said Blondin, "that instead of a sack of cement, I could put a *man* in this wheelbarrow—a man who has never been on a tightrope before—and wheel him, without a safety net, safely over to the other side?"

"Oh, yes, sir, Mr. Blondin," said the reporter, "I believe it."

"Good," said Blondin. "*Get in.*"

It is one thing to give mental assent; it is something else again to "get in." When you "get in," that's faith, and faith, of course, is a doing word. It is not something you discuss, it is something you do; it is not just something to learn, but something to live.

We are not told what happened to the reporter, except that he probably suddenly remembered an urgent appointment elsewhere. To put your life totally into the hands of others on the bare record of who they are and what they have done is faith indeed.

But that is not the end of the story. Blondin did, I understand, finally find some daredevil willing to ride in his wheelbarrow. He tipped out his sack of cement, put the man in the barrow, and started across.

Wagers were flowing on both sides of the Falls. One man in particular had tendered a very large bet Blondin would not make it. Blondin set out, wheeling the man carefully on the tight wire, who you can imagine was white-knuckling it all the way, clinging to the sides of the barrow and not daring to look down. Blondin breezily passed the halfway point on the 1,600-foot rope.

The man on the other bank who had made the large bet knew that unless something drastic happened he was surely going to lose a fortune. Surreptitiously he slipped away. He went to one of the support ropes that kept the main tightrope taut and stopped it from all side-to-side movement. And when no one was looking, he cut it.

Twa-ang! Suddenly this tensioning rope flew free. Blondin still had his man in the barrow, with many feet to go. There they were, 160 feet above the water, with Blondin's tightrope vibrating violently like a plucked bowstring. The wheelbarrow pitched crazily from side to side. Any moment now, the rim of the wheel would come off the rope. With no safety net both men would be pitched into the raging grave of Niagara Falls below.

Blondin's brave passenger was now out of his mind with fear, screaming bloody murder, and they were only seconds away from death. Then Blondin spoke, and his voice snapped like that of a military commander.

"*Stand up!*" he commanded the terrified man. "Stand up! Grab my shoulders!"

The man stared at him in unbelieving desperation.

"Let go and stand up! Let go the wheelbarrow! Do it or die!"

In total terror, the man somehow let go and fought his way up from the rocking barrow.

"Your arms—'round my neck! Now, your legs—'round my waist!"

What choice did he have? This was life or death; whether Blondin was right or wrong, he was all he had. It was obey or die. He threw his arms around Blondin's neck; he wrapped his legs around Blondin's waist. Blondin took the strain and stayed balanced there, every trained and honed muscle in his body reacting desperately to the singing, swinging wire under his feet.

The wheelbarrow, empty and abandoned, somersaulted down more than sixteen stories into the Falls and smashed into the water to be swept away. For all I know, it is down there still.

Imagine the sheer terror of this man. He had nothing left to cling to now but the man with the power and skill, the expert who had dared the rope before, time and dangerous time again, and still lived. Blondin somehow was still standing on the crazily swaying rope, arms stretched wide and shifting every second for balance, with his passenger now locked in a death grip around him. And it was then he heard Blondin say the final thing that saved his life.

"Hold on," said Blondin. "But don't fight. If we are going to make it alive, you must not fight me. You must move when I move, give when I give. You must become one with me. *For just this little while, you must become Blondin.*" And in the reality of that command, he carried him safely to the other side.

You and I, too, have a long and dangerous journey to make. There are some who bet we will not complete it. And they may be right. Indeed, they are surely right if all we have to make it with is what we are. Martin Luther understood the situation very well when he wrote:

> Did we in our own strength confide,
> Our striving would be losing;
> Were not the right Man on our side,
> The Man of God's own choosing.

The danger is real; the fall is real.

But we are *not alone.* There is Someone with us, and it is Someone who has crossed the rope—over the waters—before. Our hope, our only hope, is to hold on so tightly to Him that to all intents we share in what He is, and become part of His purpose. *Faith is not something you hold, but Someone who holds you.* We can trust Him; we *must* trust Him. And He will carry us safely to the other side.

11

The Darkness of God: Trusting When You Cannot See

I am no prophet nor the son of a prophet, but I do believe we are headed for some very dark times in this decade. I really believe in some places it is going to be rough to be a Christian. In other nations believers have already faced trouble and pressure. But what I want to look at here does not come about from the persecution of the world. This is a problem that will happen to every single Christian who wants to be involved in the work of God, or to any ordinary Christian who has set his heart on pleasing God. This is not just a problem that comes from other people; neither is it necessarily a problem that comes from the demonic world. It can very well come to Christians from God Himself.

> "Who among you fears the Lord? Who obeys the voice of His Servant? Who walks in darkness and has no light? Let him trust in the name of the Lord and rely upon his God. Look, all you who kindle a fire, who encircle yourselves with sparks: walk in the light of your fire and in the sparks you have kindled—this you shall have from My hand: you shall lie down in torment."
> Isaiah 50:10–11

When I first read this passage, I assumed it was written to an unbeliever. After all, it deals with darkness. I knew in Scripture of only three kinds of darkness and, well, everybody

145

knows that darkness comes only to unbelievers. Perhaps it meant the darkness of *sin*. After all, the Bible does say: "Men loved darkness rather than light, because their deeds were evil" (John 3:19). And again, "What communion has light with darkness?" (2 Corinthians 6:14). God has called us to be a "chosen generation, a royal priesthood, a holy nation, His own special people, that you may proclaim the praises of Him who called you out of darkness into His marvelous light" (1 Peter 2:9). "If we walk in the light as He is in the light, we have fellowship with one another, and the blood of Jesus Christ His Son cleanses us from all sin" (1 John 1:7).

Secondly, there is a darkness in the Bible that is really *ignorance*. The opposite of this darkness is the word *light*. This is one of the most basic statements of God in the entire Scriptures: "God is light and in Him is no darkness at all" (1 John 1:5).

Now this word *light* as used in the Bible means "that which is most wise." The Bible word *light* used of God says that He is the total criterion, the ultimate standard and example of all that is most wise and most holy in the universe. When the Bible says that "God dwells in the light," it means God lives perfectly according to that which is most wise and most intelligent. And when He asks us to "walk in the light," God is asking us to live according to the highest intelligence.

The Christian life calls you not only to be good but to be wise. One of the meanings of the word *darkness*, then, is "ignorance," not really understanding the ways of God.

Then, thirdly, *demonic power* is sometimes referred to as "the power of darkness" (Luke 22:53; Acts 26:18; Ephesians 6:12; Colossians 1:13). So the satanic world is sometimes involved in the word *darkness*. I've done battle before with darkness that was demonic.

But the darkness Isaiah spoke of is none of those things. The strange thing about this verse and this kind of darkness is that it happens only to people who are walking with God, who love God, who are not messing around with sin, and who are not ignorant. There is a darkness that can come to men and women of God that has nothing to do with sin, that has nothing to do with lack of wisdom, and has nothing whatsoever to do with the devil. And the tragedy is, when this darkness comes upon certain people of God, they don't understand what it is and it nearly wipes them out.

Everyone who has set his heart on serving God will have this darkness come at some point. When this happens we must learn to recognize it and deal with it.

Fears the Lord

Let's look at the person to whom this verse is addressed. God says, first of all, "Who among you fears the Lord?" *The fear of the Lord is the awesome reverence of God.*

I have often prayed that God will reveal Himself to me. When I was a new Christian, I wanted God to talk to me in an audible voice! I didn't know what I wanted Him to say, I just wanted Him to say something. I had been saved about six months so I said, "O Lord, how come You have never spoken to me? You've spoken to some of these people in the Bible. You spoke to Your Son."

I had forgotten that, as far as we know, Jesus lived thirty years before his Father spoke to Him in an audible voice. And there I was, a six-month brat, who wanted God to do all kinds of audible, supernatural things for me.

So late one night in a Christian campground I said: "God, I'm going to fast and pray. . . . I'm going to die unless You come down and speak to me. Amen."

Then I got my Bible and my sleeping bag and went out into the woods. I started to pray, "Lord, come down." I was yelling out in those woods at two o'clock in the morning. Suddenly I realized that all the crickets had stopped chirping. All the birds and owls had stopped hooting. Everything had stopped. It wasn't just that I was making a racket. I was on my knees with my Bible in front of me and I thought, *Why is everything so quiet?* So I shut up a minute. It was very, very still right then. I think I stopped breathing. And then, without turning around, still on my knees on the sleeping bag, I very slowly looked behind me. And it seemed to me that Something white was standing there.

Do you know what I did? I did not turn around. I did not dare. Without looking back, I picked up my Bible and my sleeping bag. I headed straight for my bed, got in, closed my eyes tight, and went to sleep immediately. I never prayed that prayer again. I realized that when the God of the universe appears, you don't have anything to say at all. When He comes down, the whole world shuts up. Nobody talks. Before, I had had all these questions I was going to ask God. In the morning all the answers were right there in my Bible.

This Isaiah verse is addressed to a person who "fears the Lord," who has this awesome reverence for the Lord. This isn't a cheap, shallow, one-time-in-the-presence-of-God person. This is someone who has reverenced His presence. The Bible also tells us "the fear of the Lord is to *hate evil.*" Since the fear of the Lord is to hate evil, and "the fear of the Lord is the beginning of wisdom," the one to whom *this* darkness comes is not someone living in sin or ignorance. This is a person whose life is set against evil, who does not want to do evil. This person already knows some things about God, someone perhaps who has already had a long walk with God.

Habitually Obedient

There is a second thing we know about this person: The Bible says this one will *"obey the voice of His servant."* The great Servant of servants is Jesus Himself. We may be justified here in capitalizing "His Servant"; the passage refers ultimately to someone who is obeying Christ Himself. This person is not lost; this person is a true believer. The one this verse is talking about is somebody who is an obedient follower of Jesus Christ.

This is not someone habitually living in disobedience to God. People sometimes say they are "pretty much a Christian" or "fairly Christian." You can't be half-Christian any more than you can be half-pregnant. You can only be "in Christ" or out of Him. There's no moral halfway in Scripture. God says, in effect: "There's a big, wide freeway that leads to destruction. There's a narrow little road that leads to life" (Matthew 7·13–14). There's no middle-sized motorway for people who can't make either. The Bible says, "No one can serve two masters; for either he will hate the one and love the other, or else he will be loyal to the one and despise the other" (Matthew 6:24). You can't fool around in sin or live to please yourself and still match what the Bible says when it describes a Christian.

I remember one time when I was in San Francisco. I was witnessing in Golden Gate Park. I met a young lady there who was reading something with a bunch of hip kids around her. She was smoking grass, rolling a joint. I approached. The place was so blue with smoke I was afraid I'd get high just standing around and talking. I noticed that the book she had was the Bible. That was not too unusual in those days in San Francisco. A lot of kids would do drugs and see if they could get into the imagery of the book of Revelation with all its dragons and things.

"I see you're reading a Bible," I said.

"Yes."

"Do you enjoy reading the Bible?"

"Oh, yes, I love it."

"Do you know about receiving Jesus?"

"Oh, yes, praise God, I'm a Christian."

"How much of the Bible have you read?"

"Oh, a lot of it."

"You're reading Revelation. Are you aware of the word there that is translated 'witchcraft,' the word *pharmakia?*" (Revelation 18:23).

She said, "Yes, I know that word."

"Do you know the meaning of the word *witchcraft* there? It means to induce a religious experience through the use of drugs."

"Oh, yeah, someone told me that once."

"Do you know that this is expressly forbidden in Scripture?"

"Yes, I know that."

"Then you know that using drugs is a sin?"

"Oh, of course."

I was looking at the joint in her hand that she was blowing. I said, "Then why in the world are you smoking that grass?"

She said, "You don't understand. My *body* is sinning, but my *spirit* is worshiping God."

I couldn't help but wonder which part of her was talking to me.

What is this darkness? It is something we are rarely made aware of in this hi-tech hungering for hi-touch century; it is something that the old saints and mystics often spoke about as an essential element in the development of the depth of the spiritual life. It has been largely neglected, untreated, or unknown in twentieth-century evangelical speaking and writing. It is something that comes from the hand of God.

Has it happened to you? You wake up one day to find all spiritual feelings gone. You pray and nothing seems to happen. You read your Bible, and you understand the words, but there is no light. You search your heart and find nothing to match what you are going through. You rebuke the devil, you ask others for prayer, you go to hear your favorite Christian guru—and nothing happens. No counsel seems to help; no answers answer.

St. John of the Cross called it "the dark night of the soul." Tozer called it "the ministry of the night." Spurgeon preached about "the child of light walking in darkness." The author of *The Cloud of Unknowing* wrote:

> For the first time . . . thou findest but a darkness, and as it were a "Cloud of Unknowing," thou knowest not what save that thou feelest in thy will a naked intent unto God. This darkness and this cloud . . . is betwixt thee and thy God and hindereth thee, so that thou mayest neither see Him clearly by light of understanding in thy reason nor feel Him in sweetness of love in thine affection. And therefore shape thee to bide in this darkness as long as thou mayest, evermore crying after Him whom thou lovest. For if ever thou shalt see Him or feel Him as it may be here, it must always be in this cloud and in this darkness.

Each writer dealt with this differently and on different levels, but the experience is common. It is not the darkness of wrong or guilt or demonic oppression. It is not sin; it is instead an inexplicable sense of loss, uncertainty, perplexity. It is above all a *withdrawn sense* of the presence of God.

Now it is natural to live in His sunshine. We believers don't have to sing "Don't Worry—Be Happy." We take for granted that "in the presence of God is joy and at His right hand are pleasures for evermore." Yet a lot of heaven's journey must be made at night. Happiness is not always the test of holiness. It is possible to be happy and not holy: "As the crackling of thorns underneath a pot, so is the laughter of fools," said Solomon. "This also is vanity." There is a false laughter and an empty lightness of heart that the Bible calls the sin of levity—foolishness and shallowness in the things of God and life and reality. And this is a characteristic of much of our public popular image today: Christians are often perceived as happy idiots, like people in some asylum, who are happy only because they have lost the ability to live in reality.

But God never designed real life to function in an artificial environment. Without doubt, conversion often takes place with an accompanying jolt of pure joy. In the glow of that first meeting with Christ, you get a taste of an excitement and release that seems as if it will last forever. When you first get saved you think it will be all music, dancing, and steak on the hoof. You come home like the Prodigal and there is the welcome party. But it doesn't take long at home before you hear from your elder brother who is getting mad at all the excitement over your return. The party is fun, you get a new set of clothes and a ring; but the morning after the party there'll be dishes to wash, a room to clean, and a farm to run.

St. John of the Cross, in his classic work *Dark Night of the Soul,* spoke of two levels of this darkness. The first, and the one we focus on here, deals with our attachment to the world of sense; the second, on a deeper level, with our spirit. The first dark night, which is "bitter and terrible to sense," he wrote, "is common and comes to many; these are the beginners." Even this kind of darkness, so basic to elementary solid Christian growth, is little understood today, let alone the second dark night, something "horrible and awful to our spirit" that John said is "the portion of very few. . . ."

These men and women of God are walking with Jesus. They "obey the voice of His Servant." Nothing matters to the Lord Jesus like obedience. They know this. They live in it; they love it. Then out of the blue this awful thing happens to them. Right in the middle of much glory and praise of God, there comes an inexplicable darkness. Suddenly all the lights go out in their Christian experience and nothing they do seems to change it.

What Does Darkness Look Like?

The first thing that happens is this: There's a *strange sense of emptiness* in your life. There's no sign of God. You sit in services, take your usual notes, and the message is great; but this time there is no answering chord of response in your heart. When everyone else is feeling something, why don't you feel anything?

So you pray; you get on your knees and tell God you don't feel so good. Prayer usually "changes things," it is said, but this time there seems to be no light from heaven! You go to hear teaching that has always excited you; you sit down like an addict needing a fix, stick out your arm for a Gospel shot—and nothing! You walk out of the service in which everyone else "touched God" and you say to yourself: "What in the world have I done?"

Perhaps, you think, it is *unconfessed sin.* You get on your knees and have a big response session. You apologize to everybody. You write letters of confession to your grade school teachers. You forgive your cat. You go through everything you can possibly think of, but it's all still the same. Nothing.

Then you think: "Ah ha! Of course. It's the *devil!* I haven't taken my authority in Christ." So you do. And? Still nothing.

"Well, I think I'd better go check with a Christian brother who can help me." So you go to the local godly authority on everything. . . . "Brother, can you tell me what's happening to me?" And horrors—you know what? He can't help either. He's counseled you for two hours, prayed, given you Scripture—and still you have the same darkness.

By now you are getting seriously concerned. What if you are in some really deep deception? So deep you can't even see what it is? You pray quite intensely, even desperately now: "God, *show me!* What am I doing wrong?" And again— nothing.

What you are going through is not new. It came to every major man or woman of God in Scripture. It came to Abraham when he stood waiting for God to accept his sacrifice (Genesis 15:12). It came to Moses on the mountain waiting to receive the Commandments in the "thick darkness" where God was (Deuteronomy 5:22). It came to Job when he "looked for good" and "evil came" (Job 30:26). It came to David when the bottom seemed to drop out of his world. In the middle of great trouble, when all of his enemies seemed to rise up to mock him, "deep called to deep" in David. All the flood of the waves and billows of God seemed to go over him and he cried out in agony and anger to the God whom he knew as his Rock: "Why have You forgotten me?" (Psalm 42:9). "O God," said the psalmist, "why have You cast us off forever? . . . We do not see our signs; there is no longer any prophet; nor is there any among us who knows how long" (Psalm 74:1, 9).

It came to the prophets and they wept. It came to the godly kings and they humbled themselves. One dark day it came even to Jesus the Son of God Himself. And if you set your heart to seek God, this darkness will come also to you. You will not be exempt. You will not escape it. It is the essential factor in a deep and thorough Christian experience.

Even in nature you know it's true. Nothing can live in unbroken sunshine. There must be the cycles of the night, the days of clouds and rain. Light and darkness alike are essential for plant growth; nothing but sunshine makes a desert. What is true in the seasons of nature is also true in the seasons of the spirit. Summer is beautiful, but winter must always come. Don't be surprised at the darkness. Jesus will help you walk in it sooner or later.

Satan will perhaps come and use this opportunity. A world of scoffers may surround you and taunt you as they taunted other men and women who trusted God. Your own failures and weaknesses and temptations may rise up out of nowhere and you will face a time of testing to the very roots of your life.

Dealing with Feeling

An unsaved girl who had been attending a Christian college once asked me a profound question. It is just the kind of question we need to ask for the time of great trouble and testing that faces our world now. It is the question that centrally has to do with this unique kind of darkness.

She said: "Do Christians really love Christ or do they just love the good feelings that come from loving Christ?"

Good question. Do you love Jesus or do you love the results of loving Jesus? Or put it another way: Would you still love Jesus if you could feel or sense no immediate benefits?

How do you wean a generation away from its love of pleasure as an end in itself? How do you teach a person to endure hardness, to practice patience, to handle suffering and loss victoriously, to lose something precious in order to accomplish a much greater goal of good in the end? If you were God, how would you teach your child what trust really is?

Job faced the same question when his world fell apart and God did not seem to answer. Sheltered in the personal care of God, he had walked secure in the knowledge that God his Friend was also his Provider and Protector. He, too, was a man who feared the Lord, who walked in obedience, who trusted Him. Satan's challenge to God over Job was simple. He said, in effect: "Sure Job reverences you. Why not? You are his celestial Santa Claus. Take away the presents and he'll be just the same as one of my crowd" (Job 1:8–12). So God let Satan test Job. And Job came through—but barely.

Do Christians really love Christ or do they just love the fringe benefits of obedience?

Saul, the proud and brilliant Pharisee with a driving ambition to be the most holy man of his time, faced the same awful dilemma: How do you covet holiness when covetousness is sin (Romans 7:7–13; Philippians 3:4–14)? Or to put it still another way: Babies always want to see that their parents are there, but they have to grow up one day and that means there has to come a time when they learn to realize their parents still love them even when they can't see them.

And so we have the special darkness, the darkness that is the most fearsome of all to the child of God. Not the darkness of sin, not the darkness of ignorance, not the darkness of the demonic, but the divine darkness, the darkness of the *with-*

drawn sense of the presence of God. God simply takes away the feeling of His nearness. He is always there; the omniscient, omnipotent, omnipresent Lord never sleeps, and His ear is always open to our cry. But He is a God who hides Himself, a God who dwells in darkness (Isaiah 45:15; 1 Kings 8:12). Divine darkness comes in different levels and at different times in each believer's life; but it is necessary and it accomplishes much that nothing else can do.

12

Tests of the Divine Darkness

First, it tests your courage. There is something universally scary about dark. When I was little my parents managed a shop. Friday night in New Zealand was late shopping night. They put us kids to bed early in our house behind the shop with the radio on in the darkness to keep us company until they came home again about 10:00 in the evening.

My younger sister usually dropped off to sleep right away, but I was always a night owl. Lying awake in a totally dark house was fine with the radio on quietly tuned to a classical easy listening program. But this particular night the station changed its format.

There I am in bed, trying to get to sleep, when the announcer introduces a new horror show: "Blood On the Cat"! It opens with the purported taped account of a reporter who has been murdered while spending the night on a dare in the darkness of a waxworks museum. The show opens with a courtroom full of people listening to his last recorded words. He is giving his impressions of the room in which they found him dead with the tape still running.

For the first five minutes he is full of bravado, thinking out loud. And there I am, also alone in my totally darkened room.

The reporter is looking at the wax statues: "There is Franken-stein's monster," he says. "There is the axe-murderer. Over there in the corner is Jack the Ripper."

Now I have lived in my bedroom a long time, but tonight it has become the Twilight Zone. The man is talking terror, and now everything in the room is starting to look strange.

"Funny," says the doomed reporter. "I know I'm here alone, but these things look almost alive."

Twenty seconds of silence. . . . You can hear the hiss of the tape. Then: "What was that?"

Silence. . . . "Is anyone there?"

The radio is only in the front room, about twenty paces away from my bed, but to get to it I have to cross Jack the Ripper darkness, get past Frankenstein's curtains, and make it safely past the axe-murderer doorway. So do I do it? Not on your life. I lie there and listen while my heart does hand-springs and tries to climb right out of my mouth.

"You're crazy," says the reporter to himself. "There's no-body here with you." A nervous little laugh. "It's only your imagination. . . ."

Ri-i-ght, ri-i-ght! I think desperately to myself. *Imagina-tion!*

More silence. Then, in the darkness, a tiny, almost imper-ceptible sound. Is it on the tape or is it in my room?

"Hello? Hello?" says the about-to-be-murdered man. "There *is* someone here!" It seems like forever before finally he screams.

My parents come back home a little later on to look in on me. They find a rigid, boy-shaped board in bed instead of a child.

There is something universally scary about the dark. Things always look better and safer in the light. It is one thing to be out in the jungle wilderness or an unfamiliar lonely city street in the day; it is something else again to be there when darkness falls. And so it is with your soul. The darkness tests your courage.

Second, it tests your convictions. When the darkness comes down, the first thing you do after you've tried everything else is begin to wonder what you really believe in. The first test comes to your convictions. You say to yourself: "I learned some principles. They are biblical. These principles work. You do this first and then this result happens. Now I've done this and nothing has happened." So you say to yourself: "Did I learn something or didn't I?"

How does God deliver us from a love for what He gave us? How do we deal with a *biblical* idolatry? How can we be freed when we are so entranced with the beauty of an idea *from* God that we are in danger of forgetting the God who yet has all kinds of new ideas to share that we cannot see?

We have all these things we know about God, and we try (as we have many times before) to put them into action. What if nothing happens this time? What if, inexplicably, the reliable thing does not work? Everything we have ever heard or thought about God comes under question.

Darkness has power to magnify not only fear but also dread—what we call *angst*. It isn't what we see that bothers us in *angst*, but what we don't see. In the light it is easy to be sure. In the light it is easy to be strong. In the light it is easy to have convictions. But when darkness comes down on our hearts and souls, we start to question everything we have and even are. "Do I really believe what I think and say I believe?"

You have said some things with utter conviction. You have said, "This is what I *know*, and I would die rather than deny it." You have been utterly sure of some things, and you have said that no matter what happens, you will never change those convictions. Indeed, that is the test of a true conviction: It is something you will not change no matter what. And then the darkness comes—and what is this? You find yourself questioning everything you were once so sure of. The worst thing is, you can't even judge your own conduct in the dark.

Third, it tests your calling. You had a sense of purpose when you met Jesus. You were chosen, you were called, you knew whom He wanted you to be and what He wanted you to do. But now comes your day of darkness; and suddenly everything is unaccountably unsure!

You ask yourself, "Did I really dedicate everything I have to God or not?" Something is happening to you that you can't track down. There is just no communication with God. No answering chord of response. "Did God really call me? Do I really have a ministry? Am I really in the right place?" The darkness comes down, and what was once clear is now hard to see.

Much of the conduct of young Christians, said John of the Cross, "has much to do with their love of self and their own inclinations. . . ." God desires to lead them further. He seeks to bring them out of that ignoble kind of love to a higher degree of love for Him, to free them from unworthy and unbefitting sensation-hungry pathways of devotion and lead them

> to a kind of spiritual exercise wherein they can commune with Him more abundantly and are freed more completely from imperfections. For they have now had practice for some time in the way of virtue and have persevered in meditation and prayer; whereby, through the sweetness and pleasure they have found therein, they have lost their love of the things of the world and have gained some degree of spiritual strength in God. This has enabled them to some extent to refrain from creaturely desires so that for God's sake they are now able to suffer a light burden and a little aridity without turning back to a time which they found more pleasant.
>
> When they are going about these spiritual exercises with the greatest delight and pleasure, and when they believe that the sun of Divine favor is shining most brightly upon them,

God turns all this light into darkness, and shuts the door and the source of the sweet spiritual water which they were tasting in God whensoever and for as long as they desired.

And thus He leaves them so completely in the dark that they know not whither to go . . . their inward sense being submerged in this night and left with such dryness that they not only experience no pleasure and consolation in spiritual things . . . but, on the contrary, find insipidity and bitterness. For . . . God now sees they have grown a little and are becoming strong enough to lay aside their swaddling clothes and be taken from the gentle breast; so He sets them down from His arms and teaches them to walk on their own two feet, which they feel to be very strange, for everything seems to be going wrong with them.

The very ministry you have seems at stake when the darkness comes on your life. All kinds of strange thoughts may come in during this time; these may very well be satanic. Suggestions may come: "I told you this Christianity business was just a big laugh. You should have listened to me the first time. Now you've become a Christian and it's a joke. If you had stayed with me you would have gone to hell, but at least it would have been fun on the way some of the time. So what have you got now? Nothing."

So you begin to question: "Did I really have a call from God? A ministry? To what?" You really begin to wonder.

Fourth, it tests your consecration. Left in the darkness long enough, the questions get deeper and even more searching: "Why won't God speak to me? What is wrong with me? Why can't I get an answer? I've tried everything I know and still there is nothing but silence. Am I really right with God?" You begin to ask serious questions about what you are supposed to be doing.

How do we know it is the darkness of God and not the darkness of guilt and sin? One key sign is this: You not only find no pleasure in the things of God; you find no pleasure in anything else in creation either. Not so with the one who has his heart straying back to the world; he finds greater delight in it. And if you are truly in the darkness of God, your mind and heart are centered on Him during the whole bitter experience. You are still thinking deeply about your relationship with God. This is not the mark of a backslider.

Fifth, it tests your conversion. The deep treatment of the darkness can go further. There may come a day when you get desperate on a level you never knew before—a level that strikes at the root of your very spiritual security. It has come to all the saints before you. If you have set your heart to be like Christ, it will come to you.

The question for you is now no longer one of being brave for Jesus, or being faithful to the truth, or being obedient to a call. The question for you now is more basic, more elemental, more foundational: "Exactly what does it mean to be a Christian? Am I really a Christian? If Christianity is true, do I actually 'have' it, or have I been living in some religious fantasy? *Am I really saved?*"

Sixth, ultimately it tests your commitment. The final stage of darkness searches you to your very depths. It shakes everything that can be shaken. It is the absolute bottom line. You are no longer asking questions about Christian obedience; you are now asking the ultimate question:

"Is there a God? How can I be so sure that there is? Is that God really Jesus Christ? And if so, do I really know Him?"

When your sonship is in doubt, the darkness is darkness indeed. When a clear sense of God's love is gone from your heart, the night that follows looks as if it will never end. You feel as though your heart is stone—dull, dead, stupid, unfeeling—when once you could jump for joy. You read the Bible and the promises don't promise. You try to pray, but your prayers seem to bounce back off the ceiling. And your favorite Christian counselor has nothing whatever to say to you that can help you now.

So here you are, as Spurgeon said, a "child of light walking in darkness." Clean as you know how to be, you have set your heart on pleasing God, and you are alert for spiritual war. But here you are, still in the darkness; there has been no word from God for a long time now.

Cheer up, child of God. You have not been abandoned! We have not been left comfortless. God has given us a word.

13

What to Do in Darkness

"Who among you fears the Lord? Who obeys the voice of
His Servant? Who walks in darkness and has no light? Let him
trust in the name of the Lord and rely upon his God."

Isaiah 50:10

What can you do to get out? Answer: *Nothing.* Nothing at all.
There is nothing you can do to get out of the darkness if it is
God who put you into it. That is why all your usual remedies
will fail, all your counselors draw a blank, all your frustrated
attempts come to an eventual exhausted end.

The darkness of God is given by Him, and it will not lift
until it has accomplished its work in your soul. Jacob was "left
alone" in the darkness "and there wrestled a Man with him
until the breaking of day" (Genesis 32:24). You cannot escape
it, but you can surely live through it, and God has told you
what to do when you go into it.

> If chosen men had never been alone
> In deepest silence, open-doored to God,
> No greatness ever had been dreamed or done.

First, do your duty nevertheless. What do you do when you
are going through the darkness? The funny thing about this is
that in this darkness, you can't get any guidance. That's the

165

worst part of it. You say, "Lord, I know that this is a hard place. But what shall I do?" Nothing. Silence.

"Well," you say, "at least show me what to do." Nothing. Yet what is this person in our text, Isaiah 50, doing? Look carefully: He is *walking*.

What is the first thing that happens to us when all the lights go out? Imagine yourself walking out of an auditorium with a crowd of people and all the electricity goes out—every single light. It is pitch-black, outside and inside. What do you do?

What is the first thing we ever do when darkness drops suddenly on a familiar path? We stop. We freeze. We do not want to move. A moment before we saw the way in the light, and it was simple, straight, and clear. Nothing was ahead to trip or interrupt us and our path was plain. Now the darkness has fallen and we have stopped.

But notice the description of this child of light in the midst of darkness: He or she is *still walking*.

And that's what you will have to do. The first thing you must do when the darkness comes is to do your duty, to keep going in the same direction you were going when the darkness came. You must continue your daily routine. A. W. Tozer has a very heavy thing to say about this in his book *That Incredible Christian,* in what he called "The Ministry of the Night":

> If God sets out to make you an unusual Christian, He is not likely to be as gentle as He is usually pictured by the popular Bible teachers. A sculptor does not use a manicure set to reduce a rude, unshapely piece of marble to a thing of beauty. The saw, the hammer and chisel are cruel tools, but without them the rough stone must forever remain formless and unbeautiful.
>
> To do His supreme work of grace within you, He will take from your heart everything you love most. Everything you trust in will go from you. Piles of ashes will lie where your most beautiful treasures used to be. . . .
>
> While in this state you will exist by a kind of blind will to

live. You will find none of the inward sweetness you had enjoyed before. The smile of God will be for the time withdrawn or at least hidden from your eyes. Then you will learn what faith is. You will find out the hard way but the only way open to you that true faith lies in the will, that joy unspeakable is not itself faith but a slow-ripening fruit of true faith, and you will learn that present joys will come and go as they will without altering your spiritual status or in any way affecting your position as a true child of your Heavenly Father. And you will also learn, probably to your astonishment, that it is possible to live in all good conscience before God and men and still feel nothing of "peace and joy" you hear talked about so much by immature Christians.

So what did God say to you *before* you went into the darkness? What were you supposed to do when the path was filled with light? What was your call, your command when the voice of God was clear? Then do it still. Do not stop because it is now dark. Keep on walking. Nothing has changed on the path except your perception of it. Do what God said for you to do before the darkness came. Do your duty nevertheless, and determine to keep walking in His previously revealed will regardless of the fact that now you cannot see. Keep walking even when the lights go out.

Second, trust in His name. We are to "let him who has no light trust in the name of the Lord." Notice: It is not to trust *in* the Lord; it is to trust in the *name* of the Lord.

And what is the Lord's name? Moses asked that question, too. This was God's answer out of the bush that burned with fire: "I AM THAT I AM."

His name is descriptive of what He is, and He is there. He is the uncreated, unchanging, unshakable God. He is what He always is. He has not changed in the darkness. He is not missing because you cannot see Him. God is committed in everlasting covenant to you. He is faithful and will remain faithful, regardless of your character or circumstances, "the same yesterday, today, and forever" (Hebrews 13:8), the One who bids you "be still, and know that I am God" (Psalm 46:10).

God says, "You are to trust *in My name.*" The most basic thing about God is that He is always there and He always will be. Even if you don't feel He is, *He is!* You say, "But I don't know where I am." It doesn't matter. He knows where He is! Trust in the name of the Lord. "The name of the Lord is a strong tower; the righteous run to it and are safe" (Proverbs 18:10). "Those who know Your name will put their trust in You" (Psalm 9:10).

You're to get on your knees and say: "O God, I don't feel You. I don't get any zap from You. I don't feel Your presence. But You're there nevertheless because Your Word doesn't change. Amen."

"If we believe not," said Timothy, "yet he abideth faithful: he cannot deny himself" (2 Timothy 2:13, KJV). "God may not give us an easy journey to the Promised Land," wrote Bonar, "but He will give us a safe one."

Third, remember who God is. Here is something else you can do: In this time of darkness, go over in your mind what God has already done. Those things aren't just little dreams in the back of your head. They really did happen; God really did do them. Now you are going to have to remember them.

Those things may seem very far off to you at this time, but now is when you're going to have to remember. Go back in your mind. Say, "God, You've done this before. You were like that before. You're not going to change now."

Remember what His character is like. When you can't see the way, open the Book and see again what He is like. F. B. Meyer said, "There is nothing indeed which God will not do for a man who dares step out upon what seems to be a mist, though as he puts down his foot he finds a rock beneath him." Others before you have walked in the darkness; they, too, have found that *faith is not something you hold, but Someone who holds you.*

Recall what God has already done in your life. What have you seen of God in your own experience? Then you said, "I will never doubt Him again. I have seen His hand, I know what He is like, and I am committed to Him forever."

Now, did you mean it? If you don't trust Him now, you will have cause to suspect whether you ever did. If you don't trust God in the dark, it would seem your faith is in light or in your own eyesight. Unless we trust in God and in God alone, we don't trust Him at all.

People in Bible times sometimes built memorials to the mighty acts of God in their history. They put up stones of remembrance, built permanent records in rock that would serve as witnesses to their children and to their children's children as to what God had done for them. Christians in the past often kept journals, diaries of their spiritual experiences with Jesus. From the records of both Scripture and Church history, we know that the God who acted in times past still acts today, no matter what we presently feel.

Fourth, there's a time to stay, a time to lean. What else do you have to do? Stay—or lean. What does that mean?

Years ago one of my friends and I went out to fish off the coastal waters of a place called the Great Barrier Island in New Zealand. We went out in a little rowboat and, ridiculously enough, took our wives with us.

It was the first and last time we ever did that. Our wives are great to have along except on a fishing trip, for three reasons: First, they knew even less about rowing than we did; second, we had two extra passengers in a very small boat; and third, they talked the whole time we were trying to fish.

Faye and Kathy were having a great time fellowshipping while Tony and I were having a greater time learning how to row. We took our boat out to the middle, threw our lines over, and waited for some fish to come along. The fish were a lot smarter than we were; we didn't catch anything except colds. For over an hour we sat there while the girls talked and nothing happened. Finally we looked up and saw all these dark clouds.

Tony and I looked at each other.

"Shouldn't we go back?"

"Sure."

The wind by now had started blowing offshore out toward the sea, so we started rowing back to shore. We rowed for fifteen minutes before we realized we were in exactly the same place. Our efforts had just balanced out the wind. Out there was only open ocean, and once we ran out of rowing steam, the next stop 1,200 miles away was Australia. It was getting darker and starting to rain. We had to take a break and then make a full effort to get back to shore.

Do you know what we did?

In the boat there was an anchor. What do you do with an anchor when a storm is blowing and you have to stay in the same place? You don't throw that anchor on deck where you can see it; you throw it out into the deep where you can't see it. You let it hook onto the unseen reality of the rock at the bottom of the ocean. Then it grips and there you stay until the storm blows over.

We did that. Hours later, wet and shaken, we were able to row back to safety.

And here is *an anchor for your soul in the day of darkness*. Here is a permit issued specially to you. It allows you to trust God in darkness. It is a command. It is an order. It is to be obeyed to the hilt. God says, *"Lean."* You can take this word in your hand and say to the Lord: "This is all I have. Here will I rest my case. You said it, and I will lean on Your love like a child." You have said you would trust Jesus forever. Now you get your chance.

What do you do with your faith? You can't see it. It's too dark. You have to send it out where you can't see anything. Let it touch the great I Am. Lean on His arms. Say, "God, I can't feel anything. But I just lean on You." Your song is going to be that old chorus: "I'm leaning on Jesus; contented am I." You're going to sing that every day until the darkness comes off.

You have taken Him to be your God; He has taken you to be His own. "Let him stay upon his God." This is His covenant, said Spurgeon; lean on it. You are not dealing with a liar. It is bought by blood. It is sealed by an oath. You can say, "Lord, I cannot be overconfident in what You have said. I do not know and I cannot see; but I can trust You and I can lean."

Nothing you go through in this darkness is outside of His love; everything is filtered through His careful, caring hand. "Who is this," said the biblical writer "coming up from the wilderness, leaning upon her beloved?" (Song of Solomon 8:5). Paul Pastnor put it like this in his beautiful poem:

> "Child of My love—lean hard,
> And let Me feel the pressure of your care.
> I know your burden, child. I shaped it;
> Poised it in Mine own hand;
> Made no proportion in its weight
> To thine unaided strength.
>
> "For even as I laid it on, I said,
> 'I shall be near, and while she leans on Me
> This burden shall be Mine, not hers.'
> So shall I keep My child
> Within the circling arms of My own love.
> Here, lay it down—not fear
> To impose it on a shoulder which upholds
> The government of worlds.
>
> "Yet closer come: thou art not near enough.
> I would embrace thy care;
> So I might feel My child reposing on My breast.
> Thou lovest Me? I knew it. Doubt not, then;
> But loving Me—*lean hard.*"

14

The Purpose of Darkness

Why is God doing this to me? Why this darkness? And how long will it last? How come when I talk to Him He doesn't answer? Why am I not getting any revelation in my life?

Probably because this is the only way God has of teaching you some very important lessons. And those lessons are basically these: Will you obey Him whether you feel like it or not? Will you do what He asks you to do? Will you hold onto the truth He's given you, whether you feel He's there or not?

You say, "Of course I will!"

How about with no sense of His presence?

It's easy for us to say, "O God, what I've just learned is so exciting that I'll never doubt it, never, never, never. . . ."

God says, "I heard that. You feel good now. You *say* you believe this; you *think* you understand it. We'll see."

You learn the principle. Now the problem comes. You use the principle but this time there is no flash. You say, "Hey, what *is* this?" When the Prodigal Son returned home to experience forgiveness, after all, he got a new suit, a ring, and a steak dinner. If he had gone out to the harlots and the pigs again, he would have been lucky to get a fast-food hamburger.

God doesn't want us addicted to the joy of returning. But does the fact that we can't feel it as before change the principle? We have to learn that. It's easy for someone to tell us, but it's a lot harder when we're going through it.

Some of you have *convictions* that God has written and locked into your heart. You think these are so strong, so unshakable that you will never, ever doubt them. Then the darkness comes and you start asking questions. Are these convictions really true or not? What you will find out is whether you really do believe them. The darkness will test your convictions. And the only thing left when the darkness lifts from your life is what you really do believe.

How about your *consecration?* You had a wonderful experience, perhaps in a service one time. A totally incredible, miraculous, fantastic thing happened. You wish you had a movie so you could play it back every day of your life. On that day you said, "Lord, I know You've called me. I'm giving my life to You. This is it. Hear me, Lord. I dedicate my life to You. Amen. I'll never turn back."

Then darkness comes.

Do you still trust Him when you don't feel Him? Suppose you have been praying for a miraculous confirmation of a *call.* Perhaps you have even asked God for a "fleece." A brick falls out of the sky, hits you on the head. There's a text on it: "Go to Africa." The very next week the sky lights up with lightning. The swirling clouds spell out a message in the sky: *Africa.* You come home from work and there is a spear embedded in your door. Engraved on the shaft are the words *Come over and help us.* And so you say, "God, I think I know where You want me to go."

Now it's only a few months away from getting the tickets and the darkness comes down. And you wonder, "Was it Africa or Australia?"

What about your *conversion?* Remember the day you got saved? You may have been reared in a loving Christian family who taught you how to love Jesus from the time you were a kid. You may have come from a family that was rotten or just plain nuts.

Or perhaps you know what *lost* means. You were once really bad yourself. You ran around chopping people up; you rode with Bonnie and Clyde. You shot fifty innocent citizens before you got saved, and those were just your friends! You had quite a cosmic change take place in your life at your conversion. Then you said, "I got so saved you won't believe it. I'm going to make Billy Graham look like a backslider!"

That's what you said. Then, the darkness. How are you doing now?

We say: "Salvation is not dependent on feelings." We tell young converts: "Now understand, it doesn't matter how you feel. Take it by faith." You said that to others; now you've got to live it yourself.

How long will the darkness last? A week? Maybe not. Maybe more. Maybe a year. How long will it last? *As long as it takes God to confirm those four things in your life.* And no amount of resisting the devil, searching your heart for sin, praising God, or any other normal thing that is supposed to bring release will ever do it, until God is finished with you.

When the darkness has finished its work in you, everything that can be shaken will be shaken, and only what is firm, real, and solid shall remain.

15

Benefits of the
Darkness

First, you will learn what you really know about God. We
live in an age in which communication technology has given
us the most advanced methods in history of gaining access to
knowledge. We have cassette tapes, tracts, books, videos,
radio and T.V. programs transmitted by satellite. We have
church meetings, seminars, teaching crusades, and home Bible studies. We have scores of different translations of Scripture and access to all kinds of lexicons and word study books;
we can now disobey God in Hebrew, Greek, and Aramaic.

There is danger in much light; it is not the same as spiritual
sight. It is perfectly possible, especially for us in the information age, to learn spiritual truth without ourselves becoming
spiritual. As A. W. Tozer wrote in *That Incredible Christian:*

> Spiritual truths differ from natural truths both in their consti-
> tution and in the manner of their apprehension. . . . The
> truths of the natural sciences, for instance, can be grasped by
> anyone of normal intelligence whether he is a good man or a
> scoundrel. . . . A man may study philosophy for a lifetime,
> teach it, write books about it and be all the while proud,
> covetous and thoroughly dishonest in his private dealings. The
> same thing may be said of theology. A man need not be godly

to learn theology. Indeed I wonder whether there is anything taught in any seminary on earth that could not be learned by a brigand or a swindler as well as by a consecrated Christian.

The difference between "light" and "sight," said Tozer, is in the revelation ministry of God the Holy Spirit. In "light" we can learn *about* God, but only when we learn *of* God are we given "sight." Spiritual light is a discoverable fact, and we can get as much of it as we want by close attention to reading, work, and study. But spiritual sight is a *gift of God,* and it comes only in humility of heart. Again, Tozer (from *Born After Midnight*):

To find the way we need more than light; we need also sight. . . . Between light and sight there is a wide difference. One man may have light without sight; he is blind. Another may have sight without light; he is temporarily blind.

. . . Religious instruction is not enough. It brings light, but it cannot impart sight. . . . There can be no salvation apart from truth, but there can be and often is truth without salvation. How many multiplied thousands have learned the catechism by heart and still wander in spiritual darkness because there has been no inward illumination? The assumption that light and sight are synonymous has brought spiritual tragedy to millions.

Because of our particular strength in the West in communications and information access, we are exposed through many means to much religious content. We know all kinds of things *about* God. But what do we really know *of* God? What are the actual realities He has imprinted eternally on our souls? What is revelation and what is just information? In the darkness, all we are left with is what we *really* know. Darkness teaches us the difference.

Second, you will be humbled. Are you the one with such a history in Christ that you are used to being the source of all the helpful and practical answers? Are you the one with the light and the way and the truth? You may be a leader, a challenger, an intercessor; perhaps you are used to telling people what to do and what is wrong. And it has been a habit of yours to give help and counsel to those less fortunate or blessed than you. Possibly you no longer ask for help yourself much anymore; you have spiritually "arrived." As John of the Cross said:

> As the beginners feel themselves to be very fervent and diligent in spiritual things and devout exercises from this prosperity (although it is true that holy things of their own nature cause humility), there often comes to them through their imperfections a certain degree of secret pride which they come to have with their works and with themselves. And hence there comes to them likewise a certain desire, which is somewhat vain and at times very vain, to speak of spiritual things in the presence of others and sometimes even to teach such things rather than learn them.

How can you tell the difference between what you have really learned and what you have simply passed on as information to others that you have enjoyed without embracing? You need God to show us what is truly yours in Him and what is only mental assent. And so, the darkness. You are in real need yourself now; but now you don't know what to do or what to say. The "one with all the answers" has no answer for his or her own life. Darkness comes to reveal our need of God and God alone. Don't fret over your helplessness, your emptiness; they will be riches to you. God says, "I will give you the treasures of darkness" (Isaiah 45:3).

There is more than one kind of fast in the Bible. There is also the fast in which we set our hearts under God to cut ourselves off from religious unreality, to determine to act in truth and compassion, and from the brokenness of our own lives feed others. "If you extend your soul to the hungry and satisfy the afflicted soul, then your light shall dawn in the darkness, and your darkness shall be as the noonday" (Isaiah 58:10).

Third, you will learn again the feelings of the lost. Do you remember what it felt like when you were lost from God? Perhaps you don't. Some of us have been saved so long that we don't know anymore what it's like to be lost. We have nothing now to say to a broken, hurting street kid. People may be dying in front of us, but we've forgotten what it felt like.

How is God going to teach us what it's like to be lost? What does a sinner go through each day? No conscious sense of the presence of God. God is going to have to teach us compassion, and the darkness of God will teach us well. When it is finished, we will learn again the feelings of those outside the Light of the world. And next time we talk to a lost man we'll be able to say, "I know what you feel like. I really know."

I went to work for a summer years ago at Teen Challenge in New York. I had grown up in New Zealand near a beach—a really beautiful country. A murder in New Zealand when I was a child was something nationally shocking that we seemed to hear about once in a blue moon. A generation ago, New Zealand hotels rarely even had locks on the doors.

Can you imagine coming from New Zealand for the first time to a big city like New York? I mean inner-city, run-down-ghetto, gang-warring New York in the summer. There was a murder every eighteen hours in the city then, a major robbery every three minutes. Like many a huge metropolis with gangs, drugs, and violence, New York was Paranoia City at night.

And there I was trying to minister in the heart of the city's worst crime districts. You went up to somebody to ask directions and they thought you were going to mug them. Nobody looked at you on the street; everyone walked fast in case you were a panhandler, a lunatic, or a desperate drug addict.

A friend of mine from New Zealand once visited New York.

He parked his car outside a police station, put his camera underneath the seat, locked the doors, and went in to ask directions. When he came out just a few minutes later, there was a hole smashed in the back of the car window and his camera was ripped off. In horror he ran back inside and exclaimed to the officer, "Hey, my camera got stolen! I had it under the seat of my car parked right outside."

"Too bad," the policeman said.

"What do you mean, too bad? Aren't you going to find it?"

"You've got to be kidding."

Then my friend snapped, "I demand to see the chief of police."

But when he eventually got to see him, the chief of police said the same thing. My friend got so angry he stormed out— only to discover someone had stolen his car.

So there I was in the middle of New York, feeling I just couldn't take it anymore.

I remember walking one hot, dangerous night in all this filth and I said to God: "Lord, this is ridiculous. I can't stay in this place. I can't even breathe here without eventually dying. I'm used to home with beaches and blue skies and white clouds where you can lie down right on the grass . . . no snakes to bite you, no human snakes to jump on you. And you don't get beaten up or mugged just because you have change in your pocket.

"Lord," I said, "this is it. New York is a filthy place. I can't stand it."

And then this poem I had heard one time came burning back into my mind:

> I said, "Let me walk in the fields."
> God said, "No, walk in the town."
> I said, "But there are no flowers here."
> He said, "No flowers, but a crown."
> I said, "But the sky is black.
> There is nothing but noise and din."

But He wept as He sent me back;
"There is more," He said,
"There is sin."

Do you remember what it was like to be cut off from the
love of God? To wake up each morning without a sense of
God's forgiveness, of divine purpose and security and hope?
Perhaps you met Christ years ago. It has been a long time
since you felt the wonder of that first love. You have said you
want to have His compassion for unsaved people. Perhaps you
have prayed that God would give you a heart for the lost.

And then came this darkness. You cannot feel or sense the
presence of God anymore. You wake up in the morning without any conscious sense of His nearness and His care. You no
longer are sure He is speaking to you.

Do you know what it's like to be without Christ? Darkness
will teach you. You will learn what you really know about
God. God can come at the end of darkness and comfort you in
an incredible way, but during that time you will have learned
what you really know about Jesus. You'll learn the difference
between feeling and doing, feeling and obeying. Nothing matters to Christ like obedience. You had forgotten what it was
like to be lost, but now you know again.

The darkness of God teaches us to care.

Fourth, you will prove the power of prayer. "If you always
have bread," said Spurgeon, "you'll never know the power of
the prayer 'Give us this day our daily bread.' "

If a man sneers at prayer and tells you the name of a dozen
cynical philosophers who say they prayed and God did not
answer their prayer, *believe it;* God doesn't have to answer
the prayers of professional cynics.

Jonah, the prophet, like all of us, knew something of per-
functory prayer. A man of God, he no doubt dutifully put in
his daily devotional time. Then one day God told him to "arise
and go to Ninevah." He arose and went, all right (so far, so

good!)—to Tarshish. (Not so good!) After a short and scary voyage in a vessel targeted for divine interruption, Jonah was pitched overboard and got to spend three days and nights in the belly of Jaws Five. You can bet he really learned to pray! The last thing he remembered as he dropped beneath the surface of the sea was a rush of water, a huge open mouth, and a certain sinking feeling that he was really out of the will of God.

Thank God for obedient whales. The fish didn't say to God, "O God, you know I can't stomach preachers!" And Jonah went down whole. When he finally woke up he was in a place that was dark and hot. Can you guess what he was thinking? "I knew I was a bad preacher, Lord, but I didn't know I was this bad!"

Scripture records the essence of his prayer: "Out of the belly of hell I cried, and You heard my voice." And with weeds wrapped around his neck he *really* learned to pray. For three days and three nights he prayed. He did nothing but pray—past "short" requests and "important" requests and "quite urgent" requests into *absolutely desperate* requests, the sort of life-or-death agonizing that the impending destruction of an entire city is all about. And in the School of the Whale's Stomach Jonah probably learned more about reality in prayer than he ever had in Bible college.

His eventual obedience resulted in the largest recorded awakening in the Bible: an entire city humbling itself, repenting and turning to God.

Fifth, you will come out into a greater light. Darkness often follows great light. The darkness of God often comes immediately after some of the best teaching and deepest revelation you have ever had. Like the fact that your greatest time of temptation sometimes strikes right after your most wonderful time in the things of God, spiritual darkness follows hard on the heels of a time when you have learned much.

As children my sister and I sometimes rode into town with

our relatives by train. Earlier New Zealand railcars had no lights on in the daytime. When one entered a short tunnel, the carriage where children sat became for a brief time totally dark.

You know what happens in such darkness. The pupils of your eyes, which in the sunshine had shrunk almost to pinpoints, now expand wider and wider in the darkness. And when the train suddenly bursts out of the other side of the tunnel, the brightness of the world outside is astonishing.

And so with the darkness of God. We do not know or appreciate the brightness of the light we already walk in until we enter this discipline of God. We have absorbed so much that our spiritual perception has shrunk to a pinpoint. We have been given so much that we cannot appreciate what has been shown us. And then God puts us like children onto His train and runs it into the darkness.

This darkness you are in is only a tunnel. The train is on a sure journey. It is headed without fail to the place you need to be, and the Engineer knows all of the way. The tunnel is not eternal. You will not remain in darkness forever. And you will come out of the darkness into a greater sense of light than you had when you went in. "Unto the upright there arises light in the darkness" (Psalm 112:4).

The Danger of False Fire

I want to show you what God can teach you in darkness, and then give you a beautiful promise. But first a *warning*.

"The way in which they are to conduct themselves in this night of sense," said St. John of the Cross, "is not to devote themselves to reasoning and meditation, since this is not the time for it, but to allow the soul to remain in peace and quietness, although it may seem clear to them that they are doing nothing, and are wasting their time, and although it may appear to them that it is because of their weakness that they have no desire in that state to think of anything. The truth is that they will be doing quite sufficient if they have patience and persevere in prayer without making any effort."

Isaiah 50 contains a solemn warning. You cannot take matters into your own hands. If God does not bring you light, you must not make your own. Some have tried to do just that. "If God is not going to speak," they say in anger, "then I am going ahead anyway. If He won't show me the light, I will make my own." What they are saying is, "O.K., God, if You're not going to guide me, I'm going to guide myself."

"Sparks," says the Lord. What you have then is an extremely brief and temporary light; it cannot last and will only leave you blinded. Don't do it. Don't make the foolish and futile mistake of lighting your own fire. If God has put you into the darkness, let it do its work in your soul. He got you in; you can trust Him to take you out. If you light your own light, your little match, and go and do your own thing, you will see in that manmade light a destruction of much that is beautiful that God had for you.

You cannot afford to do your own thing if you do not feel the presence of God. Walk in what God has already given you to do and remain faithful until new light comes. Light your own path and you can expect nothing but grief. You say, "No light. O.K. I'll light my own fire." Then this will be your swan song: "I did it my way."

The Bible has a word for you: "Walk in the light . . . you have kindled—This you shall have from My hand: *You shall lie down in torment*" (Isaiah 50:11).

Wrote St. John:

Spiritual persons suffer great trials; not so much of the aridities which they suffer, as of the fear which they have of being lost on the road, thinking that all spiritual blessings are over for them and that God has abandoned them since they find no help or pleasure in good things. . . .

These souls turn back at such a time if there is none who understands them; they abandon the road or lose courage; or at least they are hindered from going further by the great trouble which they take in advancing along the road of meditation and reasoning. Thus they fatigue and overwork their nature, imagining they are falling through negligence or sin. But this trouble that they are taking is quite useless; for God is now leading them by another road. . . .

It is well for those who find themselves in this condition to take comfort, to persevere in patience and to be in no wise afflicted. Let them trust in God, who abandons not those who seek Him with a simple and right heart, and will not fail to give them what is needed for the road, until He brings them into the pure and clear light of love.

God is the One who dwells in thick darkness (Deuteronomy 5:22). The darkness and the light are alike to Him (Psalm 139:12). There are treasures that can be found only in such darkness and He will show you there things about Himself and about yourself that you will never learn any other way.

And the things you will find in that darkness! You will hear the voice of God at the end of the tunnel saying, "Well done, you good and faithful servant. Enter into the joy of your Lord." You will go through it, beloved; make the most of it. He will speak to you in that very silence.

We must ask God for courage to go through the darkness ahead. This is necessary because God is going to prepare His people to obey no matter how they feel. And we must have it. Christians are going through this darkness now.

On my grandfather's wall for many years hung a small plaque. I was not a Christian when I first read it, nor then was my grandfather. Many years later, on that first night Granpoppy came to hear his oldest grandchild preach, he responded to the invitation to surrender everything to Jesus. Only a short time later he died. His house was eventually sold. I don't know what happened to that little plaque, but I still remember what it said:

I said to the man who stood at the gate of the years,
"Give me a light that I may walk safely into the unknown."
He said to me, *"Go out into the darkness*
And put your hand into the hand of God
And He shall be to you brighter than a light
And safer than a known way."

Prayer

Heavenly Father, we praise You for the light of God. We thank You for Jesus Christ, the Light of the world. We thank You, O God, that on a rainy day the sun has not vanished, just gone behind a cloud. We thank You also, O God, for the night, because plants need the darkness as well as the light to survive.

Father, we forget that we're the planting of God. We want sunshine all the time and we forget that nothing but sunshine makes a desert. Teach us, dear God, the meaning of the darkness. We don't care, Lord God. You can run us through as much darkness as we can possibly bear so long as it's not from the devil and it's not from sin. Prepare your saints, O God, for the dark times that will come by giving them a taste of what it's like not to feel Your presence and yet obey. And we thank You that we can learn a lesson of faith that will last for eternity.

Dear God, we pray for those right now who are going through times of darkness and have not understood. They have lit their own lights and gone out their own way and seen much destruction and sorrow. We hear the awful warning of Your Word: "From My hand: You shall lie down in torment." We pray, O God, that You will minister to those. Give them another chance, O Lord, and this time encourage them to go through in faith.

We pray, O Lord, for those going through times of darkness—who have felt no blessing, experienced no excitement. Nothing seems to move them, yet they've checked their hearts again and again to see if they have walked away from You and found nothing. Dear Lord, encourage their hearts. Give them a great and mighty challenge to go through this time and to learn their lesson from You.

In the name of Jesus we pray. Amen.